Brand Strategy

JOHN M. MURPHY

Brand Strategy

Published in association with the Institute of Directors

Prentice Hall
New York   London   Toronto   Sydney   Tokyo   Singapore

Published in the United States of America by
Prentice Hall Inc.
440 Sylvan Avenue
Englewood Cliffs, NJ 07632, USA
A division of Simon & Schuster International Group

Published in Great Britain by Director Books
an imprint of Fitzwilliam Publishing Limited
Simon & Schuster International Group
Fitzwilliam House, 32 Trumpington Street
Cambridge CB2 1QY, England

First published 1990

© John M. Murphy, 1990

The views of the author do not necessarily represent those of the Council of
the Institute of Directors.

Certain names used in this book may be registered trade marks in some
countries but generic names in others. The use of a name in one form or the
other implies no judgement as to its legal status in any particular country.

Library of Congress Cataloging-in-Publication Data
Murphy, John M., 1944–
    Brand strategy / John M. Murphy.
        p.   cm.
    "Published in association with the Institute of Directors."
    Includes bibliographical references.
    ISBN 0-13-084161-7
    1. Business names—United States.   2. Trademarks—United States.
    3. Brand name products—United States.   I. Title.
    HD69.B7M78   1990
    658.8'27—dc20   90-32582
                                                        CIP

Designed by Geoff Green
Typeset by Hands Fotoset, Leicester, England
Printed in Great Britain by BPCC Wheatons Ltd, Exeter, England

1 2 3 4 5 94 93 92 91 90

Contents

Contents

Contents

Contents

Contents

Preface

Preface

Brands and branding have received increasing attention in recent years and it seems certain that the interest will continue and, indeed, strengthen. Much of the interest, however, has been on the part of investors and predators, manifesting itself in the shape of 'mega-bids' (e.g. Grand Metropolitan's takeover of Pillsbury and Nestlé's of Rowntree), enhanced share prices for brand-rich companies and press speculation as to the next takeover target. While this storm has raged around them, those involved in brand management – brand managers, management accountants, trade mark agents, etc. – have continued their work much as before. Although generally they have enjoyed the increased attention that brands have been receiving (and, it must be said, from a largely unexpected quarter), it has had little direct impact on their day-to-day activities.

This is sure to change quite quickly: over the next few years auditors and accountants will find a solution to the current 'brands on the balance sheet' controversy. Although the 'solution' is likely to be a rather uneasy compromise of some sort, the current enhanced interest in brands on the part of investors and predators will be replaced by an altogether more matter-of-fact approach once brands become viewed as familiar assets of worth alongside property, stocks, investments, plant and so forth.

Even though attention will inevitably switch to elsewhere, branding and brand management will never be the same again. Once brands are recognised as being specific, separable assets of potentially great worth, the stewardship of these assets becomes much more important. This book discusses brand valuation and the current 'brands on the balance sheet' debate but it is chiefly about better brand management, a subject which will become of major importance in the 1990s and beyond.

Although any faults in the book are my own, I should like to acknowledge not only the assistance that my colleague Janet Fogg, a practising trade mark agent, gave me in the preparation of the chapter dealing with the law of trade marks, but also, the help given me by Edward Buchan and Alastair Brown of Hill Samuel on the complex subject of the role of brand valuations in mergers and acquisitions. My thanks also go to Eileen Chandler who typed the manuscript and to Sue Ridley who helped me considerably during the book's production. Finally, I must acknowledge the assistance of all my colleagues at the Interbrand Group in the development of methodologies and procedures for the analysis and evaluation of brands.

Recently, a delegate at a major marketing conference commented that if a conference imparted only one major new idea then it was well worthwhile. I hope that this book provides you with one or two important new ideas on brands, brand strategy and brand management.

John Murphy
London, 1990

1
What is a brand?

A brand is the product or service of a particular supplier which is differentiated by its name and presentation. Thus any manufacturer can produce a cola drink but only The Coca-Cola company can produce Coke.

In practice, of course, with high levels of sophistication in manufacturing and product development, many products can be produced to a virtually identical specification and at much the same price by a host of suppliers. There seems little doubt that hundreds, even thousands of suppliers around the world could produce a high quality cola syrup and put in place the bottling systems and distribution infrastructure required to bring a cola drink to market. No doubt Coca-Cola, the world leader in cola drinks, has its own special product formulation as well as particular organisational and managerial skills. Nonetheless, the major differentiating feature possessed by Coca-Cola, and the only feature which a determined and well resourced competitor would be unable convincingly to replicate, is the brand itself.

Over the years, the trade marks Coca-Cola and Coke have been developed skillfully and at enormous cost so as to embrace a set of values which go way beyond mere labelling. While an essential part of the promise of the Coke brand is concerned with taste and refreshment (and these attributes can be readily delivered by competitive products), the Coke brand in addition stands for a complex of other, less tangible benefits including consistent quality, sophistication, pleasure and relaxation. It is these further benefits, unique to the Coke brand that competitors are unable to replicate even though certain competitors, particularly the Pepsi-Cola brand, offer a product which in its formulation and brand positioning is very similar to Coke and which, therefore, delivers many of the same benefits as Coke. The particular benefits and satisfactions delivered by the Coke brand no doubt are appreciated differently from one consumer to the next and from one culture to the next. A European teenager specifying a Coke may well be particularly attracted to the sophisticated and gregarious attributes of the brand. A teenager in a Third World country may be particularly attracted by the 'American' appeal of the drink. Nonetheless, the overall personality of, and satisfactions delivered by, the Coke brand are remarkably consistent on an international basis.

A brand then is a complex thing. Not only is it the actual product, but it is also the unique property of a specific owner and has been developed over time so as to embrace a set of values and attributes (both tangible and intangible) which meaningfully and appropriately differentiate products which are otherwise very similar.

The term *gestalt* has been used to help explain the complex nature of brands. It means literally 'form' or 'shape' and the concept behind the *gestalt* is that nothing is simply the sum of its individual parts. Thus any attempt to analyse the whole by breaking it down into its molecular components is certain to fail. In psychology the term has been adopted to explain the process of perception: of how we understand and give form to the messages that we receive through our senses. A baby does not initially understand that the shapes it sees around it are people. Once it does, however, it is able to take small scraps of information (a brief glimpse of a hand, or the smell of a particular fragrance) and conjure up from these limited sensory perceptions an overall form or *gestalt*. Psychologists have suggested that much of learning – of absorbing, ordering and understanding data – consists of forming *gestalt*s, of creating patterns of understanding such that fragmentary data can be formed into a fuller, richer whole. It has also been suggested that even the most simple *gestalt*s which we respond to and which we rely upon in making sense of complex reality, need to be established over an extended period of time.

A brand, then, acts as a *gestalt* in that it is a concept which is more than the sum of its parts and which takes a long time to establish in the minds of consumers. Of course, in order to embrace a complex set of beliefs and values and internalise them as a *gestalt* the recipient (or consumer) needs to recognise that what is on offer is appropriate and attractive. In other words, the *gestalt* needs to be credible, coherent and attractive, supported and developed over time and not subject to rapid fluctuations in message, quality, positioning or overall 'mood'. The Coke brand obviously meets these criteria – Coke is tasty, attractive, offers good value and has a generalised set of intangible values which are believable and appealing. The consumer, therefore, is prepared – given exposure to and confidence in the brand – to impart to the brand an authority and unity, a cohesion, which functions as a *gestalt* prompting recognition, confidence and easy familiarity.

Not all brands, of course, gain such authority and stature in the minds of consumers. They may have no particular features which set them apart from similar brands; or quality or positioning may vary so much that the consumer lacks confidence in the brand or fails to comprehend what the brand stands for. Alternatively, of course, the personality of the brand may simply be unattractive or unconvincing. To be successful, brands must be appealing and be maintained in good shape by their owners so as to continue to satisfy the consumer's needs. A brand is therefore a 'pact' between the owner and the consumer: it allows the consumer to shop with confidence in an increasingly complex world, and it provides the owner with higher volumes, often higher margins and greater certainty as to future demand.

The development of branding

Branding is not a new phenomenon. Indeed, it has been with us since earliest times as producers have always wanted to identify uniquely the fruits of their labours, and customers have never been slow to appreciate that they prefer one producer's products to those of another. In the last one hundred years, however, the use of branding has developed considerably.

1. Legal systems have recognised that brands and other forms of intellectual property are property in a very real sense. Currently, over 160 countries have trade mark laws which allow owners of brands to claim title in their brand names and logos through trade mark registration. Owners of brands, therefore, can enjoy title to a property which is every bit as strong as the title they enjoy to more tangible forms of property such as plant and freehold estate.

3

2. The concept of branding has successfully been extended from goods to services; indeed, in countries such as the United States and those of Western Europe the rate of growth in branded services now outstrips that in branded goods. Legal systems now recognise this and make specific provision for the registration of service trade marks. The United Kingdom, for example, a relative late-comer in this respect, introduced legislation to allow the registration of service trade marks in 1986.

3. As consumer choice has grown, as marketplaces have become more crowded, and as new products have been aimed at increasingly tightly targeted sectors, intangible factors have come to play an increasingly important role in brand selection. Of course quality or, in the case of service brands, the delivery of a superior quality service, is essential to brand success, and no successful brand can exist without satisfying the needs of consumers. Nonetheless, additional intangible elements are often critical in persuading the consumer to choose between alternative branded products or services, all of which are broadly capable of satisfying his or her requirements. Modern branding is therefore concerned increasingly with the intangible elements of a brand, with assembling and maintaining in a brand a mix of attributes, both tangible and intangible, which are relevant and appealing, and which meaningfully and appropriately distinguish one brand from another.

Successful branding

The key elements in a brand are the product itself, its pricing, distribution, packaging, brand name, promotion and its overall look and presentation. It is far more that just a product – it is the particular, differentiated product of one supplier. Creating a successful brand entails blending all these various elements together in a unique way – the product or service has to be of high quality and appropriate to consumer needs, the brand name must be appealing and in tune with the consumer's perception of the product, the packaging, promotion, pricing and all other elements must similarly meet the tests of appropriateness, appeal and differentiation.

The last factor, differentiation, is of critical importance in today's crowded markets. It is not inconceivable that any one of a dozen manufacturers of confectionery and chocolate products could, with a certain difficulty and expense, produce a passable imitation of a Kit-Kat chocolate bar. They would probably have to invest in special equipment and, not enjoying Rowntree's economies of scale, they would probably also have to sacrifice margin in order to meet Rowntree's price. Nonetheless, the Kit-Kat product is not protected by patents or by any unique technology and it seems almost certain that competitors could quite closely match the Kit-Kat product in terms of the product itself, its price and so forth. Rowntree's rights are, of course, protected through its trade mark and device mark registrations and at common law, and the company could also rely on more generalised legal protection for its intellectual property rights through 'passing off' or, in certain jurisdictions, unfair competition laws. Nonetheless, these rights would only stop blatant infringements of Rowntree's rights, not broad imitation. Could not a powerful competitor develop an approximate facsimile of the Kit-Kat bar and take away some of Rowntree's market?

Such competition takes place all the time. Perrier, for example, opened up a market for bottled water in the United Kingdom, the United States and elsewhere and a host of competitive products quickly appeared. McDonald's launched its successful hamburger chain into the United Kingdom and the indigenous Wimpy chain quickly abandoned its established and rather unsuccessful retailing formula in favour of a close approximation to McDonald's retailing formula.

Nonetheless, successful competition in the branded goods sector does not consist of developing close facsimiles of existing products, though no brand owner who opens up a new product sector can expect to remain free from competition for long. Perrier, therefore, now competes with Highland Spring and a score of others, and Kit-Kat with innumerable other confectionery brands. Even Kellogg's Corn Flakes, a formidably powerful brand, faces competition from other Kellogg's brands as well as from other breakfast cereal producers.

There is an obvious need for manufacturers to compete effectively in key market sectors. When a competitor gains market share through the establishment of a new and successful product competitors must try to respond in a way which is credible and appealing to the consumer. Normally, however, this process should stop short of launching a new product which is a more-or-less undifferentiated pastiche of the original competitive product as such products are usually recognised by consumers for what they are and have little appeal unless, for example, they sell at a substantially lower price. As we discuss later, research does tend, unfortunately, to push in the direction of the pastiche as consumers, when faced with a new brand proposition, spontaneously try to fit new brand ideas within their existing frame of reference, tending therefore to score most highly those propositions, brand names and brand concepts which are most similar to the brands they already know. However, if a supplier merely offers the consumer a good facsimile of an existing brand which the consumer already knows, likes and buys, the consumer has no reason to switch allegiances to the new brand.

In practice, in 'mainstream' consumer products sectors such as beers, toiletries and foods, it is rare to achieve such massive product breakthroughs as to be able substantially to differentiate the brand in terms of performance ('wonder products' such as the first nylon stockings, stainless steel razor blades or even 'green' products occur only occasionally). Further, today's goods are produced so efficiently and well that it is difficult to achieve substantial advantages in quality or pricing. The way, therefore, in which the brand can often be most effectively differentiated is not through the product itself but through its packaging, name, presentation or market positioning. For example, a new brand can be presented in an entirely fresh and contemporary fashion so that, by implication, the old brand appears dull and dated. (Ford did this in the early 1960s when it introduced the Cortina; Britain was emerging from a period of post-war austerity, Prime Minister Harold Macmillan was telling the country that we had 'never had it so good', the Beatles were starting to take not just Britain but the world by storm, and the first package holidays were taking British tourists to quaint Spanish Mediterranean fishing villages like Torremolinos and Benidorm. Cortina caught the mood of the moment. It was fresh, cosmopolitan, youthful, even a little daring. It made its competitors – the Triumph Herald, Austin Cambridge and Hillman Minx – look positively staid and old-fashioned.) Alternatively, a new food brand, launched to compete with an established brand, could be given an image which is fresh, wholesome and natural so that the competition is shown up as being fusty, not quite good for you and over-processed.

Innovative, differentiated brands do not, however, need to be bizarre or eccentric. The degree of differentiation, of shift of emphasis, may well need only be slight. Moreover, such differentiated brands can do more than merely offer the consumer some transient new appeal and persuade him or her to switch, perhaps only temporarily. As Ford showed with the Cortina, differentiated brands can serve to outmode and wrong-foot existing brands. This process has been called 'competitive depositioning'; in effect, the owner of the new brand attempts to portray his brand in a fresh and exciting way so that, by contrast, the original competitive brand or brands appear dull and outdated.

The importance of brands

Brands are important to brand owners at two quite different levels. Firstly, they serve as a focus for consumer loyalties and therefore develop as assets which ensure future demand and hence future cash flows. They thus introduce stability into businesses, help guard against competitive encroachment, and allow investment and planning to take place with increased confidence.

The brand also serves to 'capture' the promotional investment which has been placed behind it. It has been argued that enormously valuable world brands such as Marlboro, Pepsi and Kellogg's are still benefiting massively from the large investments in brand-building which their owners placed behind them in the 1950s and 1960s when advertising media, in contrast with today, were cheap and had none of today's clutter. Thus the benefits of this past media expenditure still accrue to the brand decades later.

In contrast, organisations such as Food From Britain which has spent considerable sums of money on advertising and promoting its products, enjoy none of the benefits afforded by a brand. The promotions that Food From Britain mounted in the past on behalf of British food producers may well have created a generalised, short-term consumer interest in the products being promoted, but this interest could not be focused on a particular brand, the consumer could not identify specific products at point-of-sale, and the promotion could not 'capture' the benefit of the promotional activity by building up equity in a particular brand. Any campaign which merely seeks to promote, for example, British cheese, inevitably serves also to stimulate interest in German, French, Canadian and all other cheeses. Although Food From Britain may supply retailers with decorative Union Jacks or other promotional items in an attempt to identify the products at point-of-sale, in practice all such campaigns tend to be so generalised as merely to result in an across-the-board, short-term fillip to sales of all such products. They cannot lead to the development of longer-term brand loyalties.

The second key feature of brands is their strategic importance. The way in which brands work for their owners has been described as a process whereby the manufacturer can 'reach over the shoulder of the retailer direct to the consumer'. If manufacturers did not possess brands they would not have the ability to talk directly to consumers and would therefore be merely commodity suppliers to the middle man, the retailer. We discuss in Chapter 7 the role of own label brands and how in certain countries the initiative in brand-building has tended to pass from the producer to the retailer. Brands provide the brand owner with the opportunity to maintain a measure of balance in the relationship with the retailer. The brand allows its owner to prevent his or her products becoming simply commodities bought by intermediaries according to the market forces operating at a particular time.

Besides their importance to brand owners, brands also have very real value to consumers. A brand is a pact between the brand owner and the consumer, and branding, therefore, is by no means a cynical activity imposed on the unsuspecting consumer against his or her will. Brands allow consumers to shop with confidence in an increasingly complex world. The brand offers the consumer a guarantee of quality, value and product satisfaction. As long as the brand keeps its part of the bargain the consumer will continue to support it. Conversely, should the consumer not like the brand, or should it fail to deliver what the consumer requires, or should another brand appear which better suits the consumer's needs, the brand identity allows the consumer to avoid the brand and purchase an alternative.

Maintaining brand values

Consumers are not fools and have freedom to buy whatever brands they want. It almost goes without saying that brand owners must keep their brands in good repair and must be assiduous as to quality, distribution, pricing and brand support, for if the brand does not keep its side of the bargain, there is no reason why the consumer should continue to support it. Brands, therefore, cannot shield brand owners from their own neglect of their brands or from inappropriate pricing, promotional policies, distribution policies or range extensions. Consider the case of a consumer wishing to buy colour film. The consumer may well have a distinct preference for the Kodak brand but if it is over-priced or unavailable, they will probably quite readily settle for another brand instead. Much of the marketing and distribution function in a company is directed at ensuring that the company's brands are not handicapped by such factors and that they are available at an appropriate price, are properly presented, adequately advertised and supported, and have the full range of varieties and alternatives which the consumer might require. Given such 'equality' the function of the brand is, at point-of-sale, to tip the consumer decision in favour of the company's brand.

Even though consumers have the ability to purchase whatever products or brands they wish, in practice they are remarkably loyal to familiar brands and desert them only reluctantly. The stability of brands over an extended period is also quite remarkable. Many of today's most famous ones such as Coca-Cola, Kodak and Shell have been with us for a hundred years or more, and a high proportion of the leading brands advertised in the magazines of the 1920s and 1930s are well-known to us today.

Brands are, therefore, remarkably robust and long-lived provided they are maintained in good repair by their owners. Of course, brands have their ups and downs. Tylenol, for example, an analgesic drug produced by Bristol Myers, the market leader in its sector in the United States, suffered from a blackmail campaign against the company involving product contamination. Once, however, the campaign ended and the company had introduced new tamper-proof closures, the brand fully recovered its old strength; indeed, the brand is now stronger than it was previously. Jaguar cars is another example of a brand which has had its problems. During the 1970s quality plummeted alarmingly and sales followed the quality spiral downwards. However, once new management was appointed and quality problems were brought under control, loyalty to the brand quickly returned, though the company's financial position was never fully restored and this led to the takeover of Jaguar by Ford in late 1989. Brands are therefore robust and can survive despite short-term adversity. Consumers, however, are not fools and will not support a brand once it clearly fails to keep its side of the bargain.

9

The brand life cycle

The life cycle theory is a popular one and has been applied more-or-less persuasively to products. It works much less well, however, when applied to brands as the evidence is that, given adequate support and appropriate brand development, brands need have no life cycle at all. This is not to say that those specific products which are sold under the brand have an indefinite life; Goodyear and Dunlop, for example, do not rely any longer on the production of the crossply tyres which they produced for the Model T Ford. Kodak no longer produces the Box Brownie; even the formulation of Coca-Cola has changed over the years as has its physical packaging. It is important, therefore, for brand owners to innovate, to protect their brands, to support their brands and constantly to review the product or products sold under the brand. But, given proper brand stewardship, the brand itself need have no life cycle.

So although the theory of a *brand* life cycle carries little weight, that is not to say that a *product* cannot have a life cycle. It most certainly can and, if unchecked, may take the brand down with it. The brand owner must always be aware of the sustainability of the brand's competitive advantage and of the relationship of the functional (product) and symbolic (intangible, image) elements of the brand's make-up to the requirements of the marketplace.

The strategy that a brand owner chooses to adopt must depend upon the stage of development of a brand in a market. This can typically include the following:

1. A *proprietary* period in which the brand which was first into a market can be seen to be unique and to own the market.
2. A *competitive* stage in which competitors begin to catch up with the functional aspects of the brand and new ways need to be found to sustain the product advantage.
3. An *image* phase in which any unique product and functional advantages have been eroded and symbolic values have much greater importance in differentiating the brand from its competition.

Brands which have survived and flourished have done so through a process of evolution, changing their strategy to maintain and build their values. Coca-Cola and Kodak illustrate how this process can be successfully carried out in very different ways.

10

Until its reformulation (hurriedly rethought since) Coca-Cola, as a product, had remained practically unchanged since the 1880s. What has changed, however, is the brand's image which has constantly been updated to keep its fresh, youthful appeal. By investing in and developing the intangible elements of its brand values, Coca-Cola has been able to maintain its market leadership despite the branded threat of Pepsi, the price-led threat of retailer own labels, and the alternative flavour threats of 7-Up, Dr Pepper and a host of others.

Kodak's strategy has been exactly the opposite. The brand has maintained its leadership and stability by leading or seizing changes in technology and exploiting them to the consumer's benefit. Kodak's image has remained much the same but has been applied to an ever-evolving product offering.

It is essential, therefore, for brand owners to be prepared constantly to monitor the functional and symbolic values of their brands in the context of the changing environment in which they operate and, where necessary and appropriate, to adapt them to meet the new requirements of the market or the threat of a competitor. Different markets demand different strategies for brands to survive and succeed.

A simple matrix (Figure 1.1) can be constructed to demonstrate the relative roles of functional and symbolic aspects of a brand.

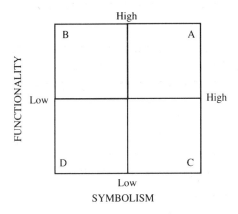

Figure 1.1   Matrix showing the relationship between the roles of a brand's functional and symbolic aspects

What is a brand?

1. In quadrant A can be found brands with high functionality and high symbolism, e.g. Rolex, Mercedes, Hasselblad.
2. In quadrant B are brands with high functionality but low symbolism, e.g. Post-it, Hoover, Konica.
3. In C are brands with low functionality but high symbolism, e.g. Gucci, Dunhill, Tiffany.
4. In D are brands with low functionality and low symbolism, e.g. Hirondelle, Tate & Lyle.

Figure 1.2 shows how some well-known car brands might be placed on such a matrix. This example demonstrates the range of possible positionings and perceptions: the 'rational' high practicality, relatively low image of Land Rover; the 'irrational' high image, relatively low utility of Alfa-Romeo; the high functionality and image of Mercedes and, towards the opposite corner, Skoda and Lada, brands which, in the United Kingdom at least, are considered by many to be neither functional nor rich in positive, intangible brand values but which sell mainly on price.

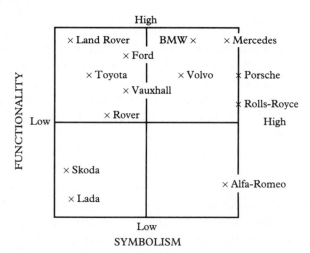

Figure 1.2 Some well-known car manufacturers applied to the matrix of Figure 1.1

The important fact demonstrated by this matrix is the ability of brands to move along one or both axes. Fifteen years ago Japanese car brands would probably have been found in the bottom left-hand corner, but by adapting their product offering to make new technology available to consumers they have pulled themselves much higher on the function scale and are now in the process of climbing up the image scale. This is the same route taken by BMW before them and which, it is intended, Rover will follow.

Ford, on the other hand, has remained steadily high on the function axis but middle of the road on image, though its initiative in seeking to acquire prestige European car marques indicates its resolve to change this.

The examination of any sector, using such a matrix, would demonstrate how brands have been repositioned in order to survive and flourish: Dunhill from cigarettes to fashion; Lucozade from sickness to health; Cadbury from confectionery to food and then back again; Brylcreem from old fogies to young blades.

The use of this mapping technique can identify the weakness of a brand in the context of its market and, through continuous monitoring, measure the success of steps taken to address those weaknesses.

Brand extension

Developing and launching new brands is normally extremely expensive and highly risky. One strategy which has been developed to reduce the costs and risks of new product introduction, to use more efficiently the equity which has been built up in existing brands and, at the same time, keep existing brands relevant and meaningful to the consumer, is brand extension. The Dunlop brand, for example, started its life as a brand of bicycle tyre but was, over time, extended to cover tyres for road vehicles as well as a wide range of automotive, industrial, consumer and sporting products. The Kodak brand has been extended from its original positioning to embrace an enormous range of photographic products. Dunhill, originally a brand of cigarettes, has been extended to cover a wide range of luxury products for both men and women. Brand extension is clearly an entirely feasible marketing strategy.

The problem for brand owners is to ensure that the brand is extended in an appropriate fashion such that the brand equity is enhanced rather than diluted. A critical factor is the development of an approach to brand extension which recognises the unique attribute of the brand and extends the brand in a fashion which is sensitive to the character of the brand and

13

plausible to the consumer. Perrier, for example, is clearly an extremely powerful brand of mineral water, and the brand possesses unique attributes of 'purity' and refreshment coupled with style and sophistication. No doubt Perrier has all the technical, financial and distribution capabilites to produce a cola or an alcohol-free beer under the Perrier brand name and it could be argued that products of this sort fulfil the key attributes of refreshment and quality which are inherent in the Perrier brand. In practice, however, a Perrier brand cola or alcohol-free beer may well be considered totally inappropriate by consumers and it may be that, should the owners of the Perrier brand wish to extend it, it could be used much more readily on personal care products, magazines, fragrances, clothing, bicycles or holiday resorts than on products which in many respects are adjacent to the brand's core area of activity.

Creative branding

Much of current new-brand development seems to consist of presenting consumers with barely differentiated facsimiles of the brands they already know and appreciate. Poor consumer research must bear part of the blame as such research pushes the brand owner in the direction of the 'bland brand' because consumers, in research situations, relate any new brand proposition to what is already familiar to them. They thus tend to score most highly those brand features which are closest to the brands that they already know. Much of successful branding, however, is concerned with getting there first, with anticipating and shaping consumer needs and desires. Indeed, there is evidence to suggest that pioneering brands are substantially more profitable than late entrants to a marketplace as it is much easier to seize and retain the attention and loyalty of consumers when there are no established competitors in the sector.

Successful creative branding consists, therefore, of thinking ahead of consumers, of anticipating their needs and wants. Consumers do not maintain schedules of new products or brands they would like to see on the market; they are generally satisfied with the brands which are currently available to them. The task of the developer of new brands is to anticipate consumers' future needs and to present the consumers with new and attractive brands which they can embrace and make a part of their purchasing repertoire but which the consumers would never have anticipated a need for in advance of the product becoming available.

Consider the fragrance market. Women do not demand from fragrance houses new fragrances such as Poison, Opium and Obsession. If they had been asked their opinion as to their satisfaction with existing brands prior to the launch of these successful new products they probably would have expressed entire satisfaction with the brands on offer. Similarly, consumers in Britain used to regard the French habit of drinking bottled water as being bizarre. Now bottled water sales in Britain are enormous and still growing rapidly, aided in large part by increased concern as to the quality of British tap water.

International branding

A further key issue facing brand owners is that of international branding. Increased travel, media overlaps between markets and the economies of production and distribution are increasingly leading to the dominance of international brands at the expense of local ones. The increased power of international brands to the detriment of local brands has been partly concealed by the development of an increasingly florid brand landscape; as consumers demand and receive more and more choice, international brands have not eliminated local brands but rather have prospered alongside them. Nonetheless, in many sectors international brands are winning increasing market share.

Besides the real economies in the areas of manufacturing, distribution and promotion which international brands bring their owners, there is one additional benefit which is of enormous importance to them, namely a coherence in their international affairs. Major brand owners now operate on far more than a national basis and if they do not have a portfolio of international brands they suffer a considerable fragmentation in their activities. If, for example, the German subsidiary of an international branded goods business possesses its own local brands it will position those brands how it wishes, develop its own advertising campaigns, plan its own line extensions and so forth exactly as it sees fit. The international branded goods business which does not own international brands acts primarily, therefore, in a central banking and facilitating role. The international brand owner who has international brands is able, on the other hand, to adopt central brand policies and strategies and implement these internationally in a coherent and controlled fashion.

This is not to say that international brands will inevitably lead to a homogenisation of consumer choice. Indeed, the successful exploitation of international brands in national markets consists of implementing local strategies for the international brand in a way which is appropriate to the local market but which at the same time fits the international brand strategy – one international company has summed this up as 'think global, act local'. Thus the move towards the internationalisation of brands is essentially one which consists of the development of international brand strategies which are specifically adapted on a national basis to suit local conditions.

Legal protection

Underpinning the concept of the brand as a valuable and important asset is the fact that manufacturers can enjoy in brands specific and powerful legal title. Legal systems afford valuable protection to brands both at common law and through registration. Certain jurisdictions also have a more generalised concept of unfair competition which affords additional powerful protection to the owners of brands. In common, however, with other forms of legal protection, it is possible for brand owners to erode their own position through neglect, misuse or a failure to establish clear title. Brands are such valuable assets that to fail to protect them adequately is inexcusable and short-sighted in business terms.

2
The significance of branding

Branding has been used from the earliest times to distinguish the products of one producer from those of another. A potter, for example, would put a cross or a thumbprint on his product to distinguish it from the products of others, and the satisfied customer would seek out the products of that potter again while the dissatisfied customer would be able to recognise the unsatisfactory product by its brand and avoid it. No doubt, too, the branded products of one potter would come to command a premium over those products, branded or otherwise, of other potters. If one potter's products were considered particularly satisfactory or aesthetically desirable, or were sought as status symbols despite being very similar to another potter's products, then the branded products would come to be more valued than others and command particular loyalties and respect.

Not surprisingly, in such a situation unscrupulous competitors are tempted to imitate, even to copy, the successful branded products of others. The world's museums contain many examples of counterfeit products from the Ancient World. The Belgae, for example, exported large quantities of counterfeit 'Roman' pottery into Britain prior to Julius Caesar's invasion. For hundreds of years Roman products had been available, at a price, to the Ancient Britons and had come to be prized by them for their superior quality and sophistication. The Belgae developed a thriving trade in counterfeit Roman pottery complete with fake brands – squiggles which their customers thought was Latin. No doubt not all customers were fooled but it had the effect of enriching Belgian potters at the expense of Roman potters. Clearly, counterfeiting of branded products is not a modern phenomenon.

Early branding

It was not until the latter half of the nineteenth century that modern branding concepts first started to be used. This phenomenon occurred simultaneously in Western Europe and in the United States and was brought about by the growth of the railways. Until the development of the railways, long distance communication and distribution by land was so expensive and difficult that much production and distribution took place on only a local basis. In England, for example, every village and hamlet had its own brewery because it was virtually impossible to transport a bulk product like beer over long distances. Indeed, many of the larger farms and estates would brew their own 'small beer' for the consumption of servants and estate workers. Once, however, it became possible to distribute beer cheaply and efficiently over longer distances, and once producers started to reap the benefits of scale production, a number of larger brewers started to dominate and the less efficient local producers were squeezed out. The consumer started to be faced, therefore, with a choice of alternative products, not just the locally produced one, and branding was used to differentiate one producer's product from those of others.

The law responded quickly to this increased use of brands and branding. Up until about one hundred years ago brand owners generally had to rely for legal protection for their brands upon legislation originally introduced to combat forgery and product adulteration. Many advertisements of the time carry admonitions to readers to 'note our brand name: none genuine without this mark'. Unfair trade practices were endemic and producers of goods applied strong pressure on governments to introduce legislation to protect their brands. In France, for example, the Union des Fabricants prevailed on the French government to introduce the first trade mark legislation, and the Union is still a powerful force today in representing the trade mark interests of French manufacturers.

The first Trade Mark Bill in the United Kingdom was drafted in 1862 and became law in 1875. The first registered trade mark in Britain was the Bass Red Triangle, a mark which is still in widespread use today. (It is also one of the many registered trade marks which have crossed the divide from industry to art as it figures in Manet's 'Bar at the *Folies Bergère*', painted in 1882.)

Many brand names still powerful and in extensive use today first saw the light of day around a hundred years ago. Coca-Cola was launched in Atlanta, Georgia in 1886. American Express travellers cheques, Quaker Oats, Heinz baked beans, Jaeger underwear and Ivory soap were all leading American brands in the 1880s and 1890s and clearly demonstrate the longevity of brands provided they are adequately supported and properly cared for. Kodak too is now a hundred years old even though the current products sold under the Kodak brand are quite different in technology, though not in broad positioning, from those produced by the company when the brand was first launched.

Modern branding

Modern branding, however, really dates from after the Second World War. In a recent article, *The Economist* observed that six times more wealth has been created in the world since the end of the Second World War than in the entire period of recorded history up to the war. Our generation has seen, therefore, a massive explosion in wealth and prosperity, and consumers in developed countries have disposable incomes at a level undreamed of only a few generations earlier.

Consumers are now able to afford an increasing array of new and different products, and producers of branded goods have not been slow to fulfil this requirement. Our grandmothers might have used no more than three or four different cleaning preparations to clean both their homes and all their family's clothes. A bar of soap would have sufficed both for floor cleaning and for washing all fabrics and might well have been used for scrubbing the bath and the front step as well. Possibly the only additional cleaning products used would have been washing soda to remove stubborn stains, silver polish and a blue bag to get the whites really white. Now thirty or fifty different cleaning products might be used to perform the full range of domestic cleaning tasks. Different products will be used to clean the bath, the kitchen floor, the cooker, the sink, windows, for woollens, carpets, stubborn stain removal and so forth. A special product even exists to restore the sparkle to crystal chandeliers.

This diversity of products and richness of choice can be demonstrated

19

by a visit to any supermarket: dozens of different branded products compete for the customers' attention. However, the products on display in a modern supermarket represent only a small proportion of those on offer from manufacturers; modern supermarkets are extremely discerning as to those products that they are prepared to stock because the available shelf space for any product or product category is limited. Generally the supermarket will stock the market leader, an own label brand and perhaps one or two other manufacturer brands. In only a few special product sectors such as beers, wines and spirits might a wide range of similar branded products be offered for sale.

The explosion of choice facing the consumer has resulted in more and more investment being placed in brand and product development by manufacturers in order to capture the attention and loyalty of the consumer. Manufacturers have, for example, increasingly developed brands which are carefully targeted at specific, often very narrow consumer sectors, although, as we have noted, producers of branded products are often inexorably attracted to the branded products of their competitors and imitate as much as innovate when developing new products.

New brand development

For whatever reasons, the vast majority of new products do not succeed in the marketplace. They are insufficiently differentiated, of the wrong quality, wrongly priced, inadequately supported, inadequately distributed or in some other way not appealing to the consumer. It is estimated that up to nineteen out of every twenty new brands fail and quite frequently the reasons for failure cannot be precisely determined. The cigarette industry recognises this phenomenon so clearly that one major American tobacco company recently likened new product development in its sector to a 'crap shoot'. It has given up agonising as to the reasons for new product failure and has instead simply adopted the policy of bringing out at least ten new brands a year and of trying to do as good a job as possible while recognising that inevitably most of the brands will fail: one or two new successes will be so for some magical and indeterminable reason.

Given such a high failure rate for new brands, it is clear that those brands which are successful, which are appealing to the consumer, which are stable and which have survived for an extended period must be regarded as particularly important and valuable assets. In a sense their value lies not just in their ability to generate future income but also in the fact that to reproduce them nineteen failures would have to be risked in order to achieve one success. Their value, therefore, is in the cost of all the failures as well as in the specific returns brought to the owner by the brand's success.

It should also be borne in mind that the cost of new product introduction is so high that those nineteen failures will have resulted in very significant losses. In Britain at present it is normally impossible to persuade the major retail groups, who control a large proportion of national distribution in areas such as food and drink, to stock a new product unless they are guaranteed that the brand will receive extensive and costly promotional support. The producer of a new brand must be prepared, therefore, to invest heavily in the new brand even though the chances of success are small.

Maintaining brand equities

Although brands, once established, can be exceptionally robust they do not survive without constant support and attention. If Eastman Kodak had not invested in and developed the Kodak brand then this brand would be of interest only as a footnote to a history of photography. Brands like Kellogg's are precisely the same; though the current product may be quite similar to the original flakes invented by Mr Kellogg, the packaging, advertising, positioning and so forth have all been constantly adapted to suit changing consumer needs and conditions. A high proportion of the company's income has also been devoted each year to maintaining the brand's interest and value to the consumer.

The benefits of brands

The brand represents, to the consumer, a credible guarantee of quality and satisfaction at a recognised price. Thus if a consumer now wishes to purchase rice of a certain type all he or she has to do is specify Uncle Ben's rice. The consumer who has experienced the product before will know that the new purchase will meet the quality of the previous product and will deliver the same satisfactions at a fair price. However, if branded rice such as Uncle Ben's did not exist and if rice were available only in grocers' shops from sacks, as it was in Britain until thirty or forty years ago, the consumer would need to approach the purchase with much more care. He or she would need to consider prices and qualities and compare one unbranded product with another. Uncle Ben's, therefore, makes shopping for rice easy; it introduces simplicity into a complex world. The use of such brands, therefore, provides the consumer with a kind of route map through what would otherwise be a bewildering range of alternatives. Conversely, though, brands can also provide the consumer with the ability to avoid a product if it has proved unsuitable in the past. For this reason brand owners must be sure to maintain quality, value and consistency in their brands.

Brands also offer a range of very real benefits to manufacturers. Firstly, they provide an opportunity for the producer to talk directly to consumers and to influence their likes and preferences. Through advertising and promotion, brands can be endowed with qualities and attributes that make them appealing, and once consumers seek out and specify a branded product retailers are virtually bound to stock it. Consumer pressure on retailers to stock certain brands is powerful and introduces a factor into the relationship between manufacturers and retailers which would not otherwise exist. If there were no brands, if retailers merely sold commodities or own label products, retailers would be able to source their products from suppliers at will subject only to normal market conditions. Brands therefore provide the manufacturer with security of demand, with a stronger bargaining position when negotiating with retailers, and with a means of influencing consumer behaviour.

In addition, and as discussed in Chapter 1, brands serve to 'capture' the promotional investment put into them, they act as a platform for line extension, and they tip the balance at point-of-sale in favour of one brand owner at the expense of another.

International brands

Brands have always shown a remarkable propensity to travel. Bass's India Pale Ale was developed specifically for expatriate Englishmen serving in India in Victorian times and was brewed both to travel well and to be refreshing in a hot climate without refrigeration. Coca-Cola first became popular in Europe during the First World War when the

Coca-Cola company determined to make its product available to all American troops wherever they might be stationed at only a nominal cost; an exercise that was repeated during the Second World War and also in Korea and Vietnam. The availability of a familiar brand under difficult and hostile conditions no doubt provided American servicemen with comfort and reassurance, and this gesture on the part of the company did much to reinforce the brand in the psyche of the American people. It also introduced the brand to people outside the United States as American servicemen were generous in providing Coca-Cola, as well as other products such as Wrigleys chewing gum, to the local population.

It is not difficult to see why brands such as Kodak, Coca-Cola and Wrigleys should have the capacity to become world brands. After all, a bottle of Coke tastes just as good to someone in Britain or in Japan as it does to someone in Atlanta. Similarly one can get just as much pleasure looking at Kodak wedding photographs in Australia as in Sweden. Basically we are all the same and the pleasures and satisfactions delivered by branded products can be as potent internationally as they are in their country of origin.

Most of today's powerful international brands were not developed as world brands; they were developed originally to serve particular national markets and first found a distinct positioning and appeal in those markets. Once established, they were then extended internationally. This process of brand globalisation has been greatly facilitated in recent years by better communications, greater travel and wider use of certain languages, especially English. With the growth of satellite television and other communication 'overlaps', it is clear that this phenomenon will continue to grow in importance as the world gets smaller. Global brands afford their owners economies and efficiencies such as those originally offered by national brands in the nineteenth century after the growth of the railways. They also offer international branded goods businesses a means of maintaining a coherence and unity in their international activities.

Brand values

Much merger and acquisition activity in the late 1980s has been concerned with capturing powerful international brands. The power and importance of brands has now been clearly recognised not just be owners but also by investors and predators. The cost of developing new brands, the risks of new product development and the rarity of strong international brands all contribute to this interest. More importantly, however, the robustness of leading brands and the guarantees they provide of stability and of future cash flows ensure that brands are now regarded as serious and valuable assets akin in many respects to income-producing property assets. The value of brand assets, however, ultimately depends on the unique pact between brand owners and the consumer. The brand owner must recognise and honour this pact and maintain the appeals and values of the brand; the consumer will continue to support the brand only as long as it meets its side of the bargain or until a more appealing brand comes along.

3
How to brand new products

New brands are extremely expensive to develop and launch. Several years of continued spending on the brand are needed before its success or failure can be ascertained. And in any case most brands fail. Clearly, new product development is not for the fainthearted. Indeed, in recent years some observers have predicted the total demise of all new product development, arguing that it is a mug's game, that far and away enough brands already exist, and that no sane company would consider any form of brand development other than brand extension.

While such doom-laden predictions are clearly absurd (they could have been made with equal emphasis twenty years ago, in which case such successful and popular brands as Apple, Antaeus, Fiesta, Hobnobs, Benetton, Walkman, Scirocco and Next, plus thousands more would not be in existence today), they do indicate the great anxiety that exists regarding new brand development. They also help to explain the high level of corporate merger and acquisition activity in the branded goods sector. How, then, should new brands be developed and successfully launched?

What should be done and by whom?

It should first be emphasised that the number of truly new brands developed and launched by companies is really quite small. Just look at the new products section of any of the major marketing magazines; you will find that most of the so-called new products or new brands are in fact new flavours or new product variants, old brands in new packaging formats, relaunched products or existing products launched into new markets. Only a tiny minority will be truly new brands.

New brand development is, therefore, a somewhat unusual and rare activity – most people in marketing will be involved in new brand development no more than a handful of times in their working careers. For this reason it is difficult for most executives in branded goods businesses to build up a body of skills and experience in the area. The result is a tendency for the same mistakes to be repeated time and again and often at enormous cost. Nonetheless, new brand development is an exciting and glamorous area. So much so that there is much competition to work in new brand development and, at the same time, a reluctance to delegate to others who may have greater skills and experience.

In fact, certain brand development agencies, graphic designers, branding and marketing consultancies and, more rarely, advertising agencies have much to offer because they have learned their trade working on a large number of projects for a variety of clients. The best of such consultancies can thus generalise about what is for most people an occasional experience. (The worst consultancies, in contrast, often appear to be little more than purveyors of narrow, even ritualistic methodologies which, at first sight, seem impressive but tend, with further acquaintance, to be closer to mumbo-jumbo.)

The first lesson, then, in new brand development is to recognise that it is a risky and costly business, that you know very little about it, that your colleagues probably know little more than you do, (if they know anything at all) and that outside advisers may be of limited help (but assume, for the sake of caution and until it is proved otherwise, that they do not know much more about it than you do). (Incidentally, if you do consider using outside new product development (NPD) consultants give them a thorough going-over first. Shop around, check credentials, ask them to explain in detail how they would handle a typical assignment, insist on plain English, insist on knowing who actually would handle your account and so forth. Then, if and when you select a consultant, prepare a clear brief with clear terms and conditions, arrange regular briefings and updates and, as we shall discuss later, do not let them over-research as such research can be extremely expensive and produce misleading results.)

The next and probably most important lesson is to ensure that your new brand has a point of difference. Consumers almost certainly have no real interest whatsoever in your new brand of paint or in your new savings plan; most probably they are more-or-less satisfied with their current brand so it is essential that you establish a meaningful point of difference which sets your brand apart from those already on the market, stimulates interest and encourages trial. Equally importantly, however, your new, differentiated brand must be attractive and credible. You could differentiate a new beer by making it green but it is unlikely to appeal except, perhaps, to New Yorkers on St Patrick's Day; you could differentiate your new shampoo by claiming that it ensures that you only need wash your hair once a fortnight but, even if such a claim were true, consumers are unlikely to believe it and almost certainly would not give the brand a chance to prove the claim.

In establishing a point of difference you by no means need to develop a brand which is eccentric or outrageous, though certain markets, such as fragrances, can present strong opportunities for such brands, as Opium, Poison and Obsession have shown. Rather, you have to develop a point of difference which is recognisable by consumers, desirable, credible and which can be properly communicated.

Developing a point of difference

Recognisable points of difference are those which manifest themselves to consumers. It is no good, therefore, basing a new brand of cola on an improved product formulation which sends the R & D department into ecstasies but which in blind taste testing the consumer cannot tell from the existing product.

Desirable points of difference are those that they need or want. Consumers want improved performance, better value, greater convenience, new and improved services and neat solutions to obvious problems (e.g. fluoride toothpastes to fight tooth decay, new types of fabric softeners which are easy to use, spray starches, etc.). Of all the desirable points of difference which you can build into your new product the most critical is *quality*. The PIMS (profit impact of market strategy) program was initiated in the United States in 1972 by the Strategic Planning Institute to try to determine how key dimensions of strategy affect profitability and growth. It has since collected data from some 450 corporations. One of the findings was that, 'in the long run, the most important single factor affecting a business unit's performance is the *quality* of its products and services relative to those of competitors'.

Credible points of difference are those which not only seem desirable and credible to consumers but which are actually delivered to the consumer once the product is tried. (Ultra Max, an American brand of shampoo, was positioned as the brand for people who blow dry their hair; the proposition was desirable and recognisable but when consumers bought it they found that it was no better than regular shampoos.)

Properly communicated points of difference are those where the brand name, packaging and, ultimately, the product and its promotion all combine to present, justify and reinforce a proposition which is differentiated, credible and appealing. (The Clinique cosmetics brand with its name, packaging and product range is one such integrated, appealing and properly communicated brand.)

Identifying new brand opportunities

How does one identify such paragons, the new brand with an appropriate and clearly identified point of difference? One thing which is certain is that they do not emerge by some 'eureka' process. Nor do they emerge by scanning the marketing or trade press and hoping for inspiration. Indeed, new brand development based on such a process is doomed to failure as many others will have read precisely the same material as you and will have arrived at the same new brand idea as you at precisely the same time. (This happened in Britain in the 1970s when every 'expert' was predicting that DIY superstores would provide the major retailing success of the 1980s. A dozen or so major retailers immediately rushed to enter the sector. A few, including Harris Queensway, got their fingers badly burned, and only two or three, among them B&Q and Homebase, have lasted the course to become serious, well-established, profitable retail businesses. The same thing happened again in the 1980s when all the pundits were predicting that light, reduced-alcohol drinks, particularly those aimed at young women, would be surefire winners. A host of almost identical drinks were developed with exotic names and 'youthful', 'contemporary' packaging – mostly with a tropical theme – but only Malibu seems assured of any lasting success.)

A survey conducted in 1982 by consultants Booz Allen & Hamilton suggested that successful new brands are developed through an intimate knowledge of markets and market trends, and a clear, objective, no-nonsense understanding of internal company resources and capabilities. Such analysis and understanding identifies markets for which new brands can be developed and suggests the internal criteria that must be met in order to ensure that the process is linked to wider corporate growth objectives. Indeed, according to Booz Allen, the essence of a successful strategy is that it must 'link the new product process to company objectives and provide a focus for idea/concept generation'.

The sources of new brand and new product concepts are many and a variety of techniques can usefully be used including brainstorming, specific R&D programmes and formal search programmes. In practice, it is sensible to cast one's net as wide as possible in the search for new concepts, as the larger the number of concepts under review the greater is the chance that a winner will emerge.

The process must not depend upon the 'eureka' factor, though. It is essential to establish formal criteria, maintain a detailed and sensitive understanding of the market, and search always for that elusive point of difference, one which is desirable and credible and which can be coherently and effectively communicated to the consumer.

Reasons for brand failure

Many new brands fail for readily understandable reasons: the product did not work, or a major competitor cut prices so vigorously that it was not worthwhile for retailers to give the new brand a trial, or the packaging was poor. Frequently, however, it is not possible confidently to identify the reason for failure: the brand appeared to be well contrived, properly priced, well packaged and it achieved national distribution. In such circumstances the most common reason for failure is quite simply that the brand had no point of difference; it was merely a good facsimile of existing brands with which the consumer was already happy, and it could offer the consumer no good reason to switch. Heldenbrau, a new lager beer brand launched by Whitbread in the 1970s had all the components of a successful Northern European style lager brand, and yet it failed because, in the final analysis, it was utterly undifferentiated from other successful brands with which the consumer was well satisfied.

The role of market research

Market research pushes in the direction of the 'bland brand' because, frankly, much market research in the new product area is not done imaginatively or well. For example, male lager drinkers are asked to list, in qualitative groups, the features they consider essential for an 'authentic' lager beer – 'it must be German', 'Gothic lettering', 'taste exactly the same as Heineken or Carlsberg', 'it must have an eagle', '-*brau* at the end', 'one of those umlaut things'. These findings are virtuously reported back to the client and new brands are developed which are mere pastiches of existing brands: the branding equivalent of painting by numbers.

Fortunately, research techniques do exist which are designed to avoid most of such problems.

1. They test new brand concepts alongside competitive products to see whether they stack up.
2. They identify and test key differences.
3. They focus on the real target market (often heavy users of competitive products) not just on more generalised socio-economic groups.
4. They work hard to understand consumer motivations.
5. They use realistic stimuli.

Such research techniques are not, however, widely used, and much current market research seems to be of little value though enormously costly.

In the qualitative area, many group discussions – a form of marketing seance which many people fondly think permits them to gaze into the soul of the consumer – are singularly lacking in depth or originality. Many group discussions, for example, are so rigidly organised and led that the session is over before anything other than banalities are discussed. Another problem is one of quality: group discussions are bought by clients in much the same way as they would buy carbon paper or soya bean futures: 'How much for six group discussions, C1C2 women, Northern England?' They are then organised and run by a junior executive with little marketing and research experience, and who, in any case, quickly tires of spending three or four evenings a week running repetitive qualitative groups and living in hotels. In addition, the research debrief sometimes seems to bear little relationship to what actually was said in the groups and yet is frequently regarded by companies as scriptural in its significance. Much current quantitative research can often be equally valueless, even misleading: the questionnaires are often badly constructed, inadequately researched and quite untested. They can produce entirely misleading results which give a treacherous and entirely spurious air of science and accuracy to the brand development project.

Branding by retailers

One of the paradoxes of new brand and product development over the last ten years in fast-moving consumer goods sectors such as food and drink in the United Kingdom is that many of the most original and successful initiatives have been taken not by manufacturers but by retailers. This development is now starting in the United States and will assume increasing importance with the concentration of retail power in a smaller number of retail groups.

Marks and Spencer, for example, has been outstandingly successful in this respect and its example has prompted other major retailers to follow. Such groups as Tesco, Asda and Sainsbury have done so with alacrity and the net result has been an erosion of the influence and esteem afforded manufacturer's brands and a further concentration of power in the hands of the retailer.

Retailers such as Marks and Spencer and Tesco normally eschew the more tedious and laborious processes followed in the new brand development area. Typically, a buyer in one of the major retailers will identify a potential new product or brand from one of many sources: customer demands, suggestions from other members of staff, proposals from suppliers, even dissatisfaction with existing branded products. (A major retailer recently launched a new own label range because the existing suppliers, who dominated the sector, were 'blithering idiots'. They had undertaken no brand development for years and the retailer knew that he could buy the unbranded product in Scandinavia, brand it himself and put it into his stores at half the price of the brand leader. This the retailer did and, having done so, proceeded to innovate and develop the sector without having to suffer the frustrations caused by an inefficient, complacent supplier.) Having identified a plausible new concept it is quite likely that the buyer will draw up an outline specification, contact a few selected suppliers and invite them to produce some trial product (usually at their expense). If the concept still appears likely to succeed, the buyer will select a supplier, have limited quantities produced and put them on the shelves in a few stores to gauge consumer reaction. If the product does succeed it will be extended to all stores; if it fails any remaining product will be discounted, thrown away or given to charity and the retailer will try something else.

Clearly, innovation of this type is extremely inexpensive. Though it occupies executive time and there are costs involved in packaging design, labelling and so on, the costs are only a tiny proportion of those hazarded by the manufacturers in 'conventional' new brand development complete with large research budgets and massive launch expenditure.

Manufacturers often argue that the retailer is somehow in a 'privileged' position and that such 'fast-focus' new brand development is impossible for the manufacturer. While there is a measure of truth in this (see Chapter 7 for further discussion of this proposition), in fact the retailer is simply following the well-informed, pragmatic, no-nonsense approach which manufacturers would do well also to follow. It seems clear, in many instances, that retailers know and understand their markets and market sectors and the needs and motivations of their customers rather better than do manufacturers. Manufacturers pore over their tracking studies, omnibus research reports and market share statistics and take satisfaction in portraying retailers as wealthy *idiots savants*. In fact, manufacturers are often quite divorced from the real needs and motivations of the consumer; the data they receive provide information but not insights. (One cynic likened the process to trying to understand Japan and the Japanese consumer by reading the reports and statistics published by MITI, the Japanese trade ministry.) Retailers often are simply better informed than manufacturers in critical areas and more able to identify real new brand opportunities; and by keeping the process simple and inexpensive they can cut their losses if things go wrong and avoid recrimination.

Even though the processes of new brand development followed by many British manufacturers can often be criticised as being unimaginative and laborious, the mechanistic approach sometimes taken in the United States can make British practice look positively racy. A new brand development manager in a major American foods group recently said of his new brand: 'frankly, I don't think it's got a hope in hell but I've done it by the book and if it fails it won't be my fault.' He went on to describe this attitude as 'taking out ass insurance'. This approach is particularly curious as, at first sight, the United States would appear to be the ideal test-bed for low risk, low cost product and brand innovation. It has well-developed local television, radio and newspaper networks which would seem to provide an ideal opportunity to try out new brand concepts in a real-life situation and at relatively low cost.

Manufacturers, then, are advised to take a much more pragmatic, no-nonsense approach to new brand development than is often the case at present. Frequently, inexperience in the new product development area coupled with a keen realisation that the process is risky and expensive leads to a gross over-complication of the process and an intense focus on examining minutiae at the expense of understanding the whole. Where then, is a fast-focus approach appropriate and where is it not?

Brand search

One area where no compromise should be made is in the area of understanding the market and the needs of the consumer. This, however, goes way beyond merely analysing and understanding market statistics. An analyst working in the tyre industry, for example, may well be able to describe in detail the market and industry trends, and may, therefore, be able to tell you that, in his or her opinion, your concept for a new brand of low profile 10″ crossply tyre is quite batty. It is unlikely, however, that his or her detailed knowledge of the market will provide any clear specification as to what exactly you should be doing. Moreover, any gaps in the market that have been discerned by the analyst should be approached with extreme caution as it is likely that analysts in competing companies have simultaneously spotted the same gap.

Sources of new brand ideas are many and wide-ranging. One source, though, which seems curiously little used is the simple process of seeing what other people are doing in similar markets around the world. Consider dry roasted peanuts or McDonald's-style hamburgers. Until the early 1970s neither of these products was available in the United Kingdom, yet Britons visiting the United States had enjoyed these products and clearly would have purchased them had they been available in the United Kingdom. It is curious that no British manufacturer, seeking new product ideas, seized upon these. The dry roasted peanuts concept would have been particularly easy to evaluate with a high level of confidence in the results. Any manufacturer could have imported a few boxes of the American product, tried them on British consumers and, if they were liked, he would already have had a good idea as to the preferred taste characteristics of the product, the sorts of prices at which the product could be bought and sold, workable packaging formats and so on. The entire process of concept development, initial product development, refinement, consideration of alternative packaging technologies, taste testing and so forth could be enormously foreshortened and, using this method, product and brand concepts could be considered, evaluated and accepted or rejected, at low cost, low risk and high speed. (In the event, when dry roasted peanuts were eventually launched on the British market it was by Planter's, part of the American Nabisco company.)

Of course, very many products popular in overseas markets will not comfortably make the transition into other markets. Dr Pepper, for example, a highly successful soft drink in America for which consumers acquire a taste at a young age, has been unsuccessful in the United Kingdom. This failure has been attributed in large measure to its idiosyncratic taste which seems not to appeal unless you are weaned to it. The British product Marmite, and its Australian cousin Vegemite, are enormously appealing in their home markets but are often considered little short of disgusting in export markets.

In spite of such products which are unlikely to make the transition into other markets, opportunities for product transfer abound. For example, only a few years ago electric jug kettles did not exist in Britain. British consumers, who had frequently seen such products in Europe, complained bitterly about their non-availability at home and the fact that whenever they wanted a small quantity of hot water they had to quarter fill the kettle; yet manufacturers took no notice and it was not until the early 1980s that jug kettles first appeared in Britain. They have proved enormously successful. American visitors to Britain still remark that heated towel rails, so popular in this country, are not widely available in America. Isotonic sports drinks (for example, Pocari Sweat), have been massively popular in Japan for many years but have still not been launched in Britain with any great marketing effort. 'Dry' beer (with a special, dry after-taste) is yet another example; originally launched with much success in Japan, American brewers have shown some interest but in Europe only Heineken is reported to be considering an initiative in this sector. Workable new product concepts abound in overseas markets – the evidence is clear. It is also clear, however, that to identify them more effort is needed than merely a 48-hour stopover and a trip to a local supermarket.

Testing the concept

Whatever the origination process used, once a new brand concept has been developed very real opportunities exist for 'fast focus' in the research and concept testing area. Much market research, both qualitative and quantitative, is mindless, inappropriate and, at times, misleading. Simple, unelaborate qualitative research can often provide valuable information and considerable 'comfort' as to acceptability and preferences. The research must, however, be conducted among the real target users – often heavy users of competitive products – and not just among a general selection of target consumers. Sponsors should also make an effort to attend all the test groups in order to gain valuable, first-hand, unadulterated insights; perhaps even running the groups themselves in order better to guide the discussions and keep to relevant and pertinent topics.

The final part of the process is to try the new brand concept on consumers in a real-life situation – as retailers have shown so well, this is the acid test. Manufacturers frequently spend so much time developing, testing, refining, retesting, reformulating and so on that the new brand concept ceases to bear any relation to reality. It is somewhat like designing a car by focusing in great detail on all the individual components without stepping back from time to time to reappraise the car's overall look and functionality.

A number of retailers provide a service whereby they make available shelf space for simple, unsophisticated but entirely real-life product trials. Gateway, for example, offer the proprietary Storetest and Hothouse testing services whereby manufacturers can test products, packs and concepts under real retail conditions with real consumers. Alternatively, particularly when security is a critical factor, various simulated test market techniques can be used. Such techniques are, however, quite expensive and in practice may provide little more real data than the simple expedient of putting the product on the shelf, seeing if it sells and then whether or not consumers come back for more.

The process of new brand development advocated here is essentially a simple process: one of mere trading. Come up with something that the consumer wants, offer it to them; if they buy it and like it then the product is a success; if not it is a failure, and time for the would-be entrepreneur to replan and rethink.

Although a pragmatic, fast-focus, no-nonsense approach to new brand development is recommended, there is at least one area where it is inappropriate but where in practice corners are cut all the time, even when expense and effort is lavished on every other aspect of the new brand development process. It is the area of name development. The brand name is the product's one component which is unlikely ever to change and which is at the heart of its personality. It is also the feature of the brand in which the brand owner can establish clear legal title. Furthermore, if there is any intention that, once successful, the brand will be marketed internationally then it is essential to establish a strong, appropriate and internationally protectable brand name at the outset. If the brand owner should neglect to do so it is virtually certain that the new brand name will prove either unsuitable or unavailable in key international markets when the brand owner decides to market the brand abroad. The brand owner will be forced, therefore, to adopt a series of local brand names for the same product and will soon have on his hands not an international brand but a medley of local, similar brands each with its own brand name, packaging, positioning, advertising and separate brand personality.

Conclusions

The overwhelmingly important factor in new brand development is to establish in the new brand a recognisable, desirable and credible point of difference. In order to find this point of difference, an intimate understanding of the target market and of consumers is essential. New brand developers would be unwise to rely upon inspiration. Nor should they rely upon market researchers to act on their behalf as interlocutors, to peer into consumers minds and identify their hidden needs and wishes. Indeed, it is a serious error of judgement on the part of new brand developers to distance themselves from consumers, prefering not to 'waste' their time attending qualitative groups, in the belief that the research company will tell them all they need to know. First-hand experience may not provide all the answers, but it does provide valuable insights that cannot be gained in any other fashion.

There is, at present, a real danger that new brand development will start to be shunned altogether as the risks and costs of developing new brands become widely acknowledged and some companies begin to consider them unacceptable. The high risk and cost of new brand development results not from the intrinsic nature of the process but largely from the fact that it is often done badly and inappropriately. New brand development will always carry some risk and it will never be possible to do it for free. Properly handled, however, the risks and costs can be much reduced, and to shun new brand development on the grounds of risk and cost is inappropriate. Indeed, in a market environment where consumers are seeking ever greater choice, major opportunities exist for the brand owner sufficiently bold and skilful to fly in the face of conventional wisdom.

4
Branding services

Mars is one of the world's most successful companies in the areas of brand development and brand management. Its brands are powerful, international, appealing to customers, of high quality and they also offer exceptional value for money. Mars manages its brands with great skill and this is manifest in the areas of new brand development, product manufacture, distribution, and even at point-of-sale – Mars has a strong team of sales staff and merchandisers who ensure that the company's products are well displayed, in prominent positions in shops, with adequate stocks and any appropriate supporting point-of-sale material. If changes are called for in product specification, or in packaging, pricing or product positioning, they are carefully considered, along with the short- and long-term implications for the brand both nationally and internationally. Any decision to make a change is finally taken centrally and communicated to all the Mars manufacturing and distribution companies. Mars is able, therefore, to keep very tight control of its brands at all stages in the branding process.

Particular problems of services branding

Contrast Mars with how a financial services company such as Prudential might go about branding its services. Firstly, its brands are intangible; though they can, and frequently do, carry their own brand names they cannot be distinguished by taste, feel, colour or appearance. Thus whereas a consumer can readily tell the difference between a Topic bar

38

and a Mars bar even though, in fact, they are really quite similar in their size, shape, distribution, general appearance, the satisfactions they deliver, their price and their taste, consumers find it much more difficult to distinguish between, for example, a '20 year capital accumulator index-linked plan' and a '20 year endowment plan with tax free roll up'. These two examples are, incidentally, fictional, but 99 per cent of the population would probably not recognise them as such. Whereas most people would recognise a tangible fiction, for example 'a crisp chocolate wafer with added sardines', recognising an intangible fiction is much more difficult: another indication of the difficulties involved in giving form, substance and identity to *concepts* as opposed to *things*.

The problems are compounded by the fact that service products are normally in a constant state of change, especially those in the financial sphere: new legislation is constantly being introduced, interest rates change, competitors reinterpret the rules to develop new, more attractive products and so forth. Therefore, whereas Mars can be more-or-less confident that any successful new brand it launches will be largely unchanged in twenty or even fifty years time, Prudential or Abbey Life may be forced to make substantial changes to its brands at the time of each new budget and perhaps even more frequently.

All service brands share this problem of intangibility, of the need by the brand owner to give form, shape, substance and personality to something which is intangible and whose characteristics may appear bafflingly complex to the consumer. Certain service brands, however, have additional problems: quality control. Whereas Mars can control the quality of its branded products, the best laid plans of Hertz or Hilton can be thwarted by a snarling receptionist, a badly prepared car, or a hotel room which has not been properly cleaned. Staff training and quality maintenance are of massive significance to the development and creation of brands in the service area, and the problem is made more acute by the fact that many of those who actually interface with the client and provide the branded service are relatively unskilled and not highly paid. If a surly shop assistant serves a customer a Mars bar this does not reflect in any way on the Mars brand; if a similarly surly sales person deals with a customer in a Hertz car rental office all the effort involved in building a brand and attracting consumers may be thwarted.

The need for branded services

Paradoxically, even though it is far more difficult to build and sustain brands in the services sector than in the product sector, the need for branded services is particularly acute and the opportunities for new brand development are enormous. One of the key functions of a brand, as discussed earlier, is to reassure consumers as to quality and origin and, at the same time, to provide them with a simple route map through what may otherwise be a bewildering choice. Thus brands help the consumer to shop confidently and unerringly.

The service sector is a particularly difficult one for the consumer to shop: the range of choice is very wide, the services and service products are often complex and each tends to meld into the next because consumers frequently do not perceive underlying structures and so cannot discern the boundaries between alternatives. The market for savings provides a good example. Consumers have an enormous range of savings options ranging from government bonds, through building societies, banks, the stock market, investment in tangible assets to the option of leaving their savings under the mattress and not investing them at all. It is clear that many consumers do not have any well-developed overview of the savings market whatsoever and often make important savings decisions based on hunch, anecdote, established family savings habits, advice from workmates and so on.

The difficulty that consumers have in exercising informed choice in the personal finance area was illustrated in Britain in the early 1970s when the government proposed changes to company pension legislation. These changes would have a profound effect on a family's long-term financial arrangements, and yet people took but the slightest interest in the new options presented to them, often making important decisions on the basis of advice given by a local union official or the person at the next desk. In contrast, consumers are often much more informed and knowledgeable, and have established much more rational preferences, about various brands and grades of washing-up liquid or garden fertiliser. In such areas as financial services, therefore, branding can provide an opportunity for suppliers to introduce form and structure into an amorphous and bewildering shopping environment. Branding also provides consumers with the opportunity to shop in a complex market with increased confidence and assurance.

40

Types of service brands

Service brands fall into two main categories:

1. Branded intangible service products such as financial products.
2. Branded services provided on a person-to-person basis such as food services and retail services.

In practice, both forms of service brands are quite different. The former is altogether intangible but does not actually consist of the provision of a person-to-person service. The second type of service brand is what most people would regard as a 'true' service brand, and is the one that presents particular problems of quality control.

The growing importance of services

As economies become more developed, the importance of services and service businesses grows significantly. It has been reported that one person in ten in Britain now works in some sort of financial services business whereas the number at the beginning of the century was around one in a hundred. Moreover, entirely new types of consumer service have grown up in the last few decades which would have been quite unthinkable only a generation or two earlier. These include airlines, hotel chains, package tours, car rental chains, fast food outlets, specialised retail outlets such as garden centres, mail order companies and so on. Business-to-business services have shown a similar growth. Overnight parcel delivery services, courier services, staff agencies, same-day printing companies, specialised maintenance firms for computers and word processors have all appeared in the last twenty years and have proved enormously successful. Western European countries, Japan and the United States are rapidly moving from manufacturing-based to service-based economies.

It was mentioned earlier how, with the growth of the railways in the nineteenth century, the small breweries found in every village were gradually forced out of business through the development of regional and national breweries which became able to distribute their goods relatively cheaply over long distances and thus compete with the local monopolies previously enjoyed by the local breweries. This development led to the growth of nationally branded goods, many of which brands are still with us today. A similar process is currently taking place in the services sector. Catering, for example, has become increasingly branded over the last twenty to thirty years. Indeed, going back even further, between the wars there were a few branded food chains in Britain such as J. Lyons, and Kardomah but these were not, by modern standards, widespread, and only a tiny proportion of the already-small number of meals eaten out would be eaten in such outlets. A large number of small, owner-managed catering businesses did, of course, exist offering snacks and meals but these had no centralised branding, no consistency of product quality and provided little reassurance to the consumer.

In Britain there now exists a large number of branded national food chains including McDonald's, Wimpy, Pizza Hut, Little Chef, Berni and scores of others. These branded catering chains, offering predictable quality and value, may well be partly responsible for the increased numbers of people eating out. It is now reckoned that in the United States more meals are consumed out of the home than in, and that the majority of these are eaten in 'branded' food outlets.

A similar shift in consumer behaviour is taking place in a host of other service sectors. Dyno-Rod, for example, recognised the market opportunity for an efficient, high quality branded drain clearing service and have carved out a powerful and profitable niche for themselves in this area.

Although branded services have, over the years, 'invaded' whole sectors which were previously unbranded, nonetheless many opportunities remain. Many services are still provided by local suppliers with their own standards of quality control and variable skills – window cleaning and care services for the elderly are examples. There seems little doubt, therefore, that branded services will continue to grow at the expense of the unbranded local offering as the assurance provided to the consumer by a branded service is altogether more appealing in many instances than the unbranded alternative. (See also Chapter 15 which looks at licensing and franchising, particularly of services.)

The essentials of services branding

Given that branding in the services sector is especially difficult, that consumers seek, nonetheless, the reassurance provided by brands, and that major opportunities are opening up due to the increased importance of services in our economy and the non-availability of brands in certain market sectors, how does one go about branding services? The most important factor, as far as the consumer is concerned, is to keep the brand proposition simple. The very intangibility of services makes it essential that the supplier of services puts across the brand proposition in an entirely straightforward and uncomplicated fashion. The purpose of branding is essentially to simplify the complex: not to make a complex world even more bewildering. Dyno-Rod has been successful with its drain clearing service because it makes a simple, straightforward proposition – if you have a drains problem we will clear it for you. Indeed, Dyno-Rod's advertising message, 'Satisfaction or your blockage back', sums this proposition up neatly. No doubt Dyno-Rod has a series of sub-brands to distinguish particular services at point-of-sale but the whole thrust of the branding is directed at a single brand proposition.

Of course, such simple and elegant solutions are not always available to all suppliers of services. In the financial services area, for example, organisations such as the Halifax Building Society, the National Westminster Bank or Citibank now offer such an enormous array of alternative financial products and services that their corporate names have become altogether too generalised to focus with any precision on specific branded products. In such situations the corporate name must be used to deliver more generalised benefits of quality, value and integrity; product brand names can then be used to focus more unequivocally on specific product benefits and attributes. Such two-tier branding systems can successfully use the more generalised strengths of the corporate name in conjunction with the more closely targeted strengths of specific product brands. Even in such instances, however, it is still necessary to keep the branding process as simple and straightforward as possible, as the consumer's interest in the product is likely to be extremely low and the brand owner must compete for a share of the consumer's limited attention. If the branding structure is over-elaborate and complex the consumer will simply ignore it and focus attention elsewhere. Indeed, it may even confuse the people who have to work with it.

Another important principle of services branding is that strict quality control is essential at all stages in the process, especially for 'retail' services. This is a particularly difficult problem and considerable emphasis needs to be placed on staff selection, training, motivation and on close day-to-day control. American companies have proved particularly skilful in developing and implementing the controls necessary to ensure the delivery of service brands to appropriately high standards of quality. Their techniques have, however, often proved quite difficult to apply in European countries. Fast food retailers such as Kentucky Fried Chicken have been dogged over the years by staff and franchisees, particularly in Britain, who see no particular reason why they should slavishly follow the rules handed down from above when they can see quite clearly that their own local modification of the brand is an improvement for which head office should be grateful. The company has consistently encountered problems with franchisees who have altered the menu or the decor without the franchisor's authority or have lowered hygiene standards. It is essential, then, that service businesses devote much of their energy to the maintenance of quality and service standards.

The growth of franchising

The strategy that many companies in the person-to-person service brand sector have adopted to ensure the delivery at point-of-sale of a high quality branded service is franchising. Under this system franchisees become, in effect, entrepreneurs and thus are expected to adopt all the attitudes and values of the brand owner but closer to the point of delivery. The responsibility for intimate control is therefore moved down the organisation chain nearer to the consumer, though the brand owner still retains an important supervisory and control role in respect of the brand. Brand licensing and franchising is discussed in more detail in Chapter 15 and it is in the area of person-to-person service brands that it has its widest expression.

Service trade mark legislation

Most developed countries have for many years had specific provision for the registration of service trade marks. In Britain, however, it was only in 1984 that the 1938 Act was extended to cover services as well as goods. (This Act did not come into force until two years later.) It had, however, become increasingly clear over the previous three decades that this serious omission needed to be rectified. Successive governments had considered the introduction of amending legislation and had been persuaded that the increased importance of services to the economy justified the provision of specific protection for the owners of service brand names. Unfortunately, though, parliamentary time had never been available to pass the necessary enabling legislation. Until 1984, therefore, owners of service brands had to obtain whatever statutory trade mark protection they could by, for example, registering their trade marks for printed matters and related goods – after all, even though service businesses such as Prudential and McDonald's do not trade in paper, they certainly produce a lot of it.

The government was finally persuaded to pass new service mark legislation by its wish to ensure that any new European trade mark system had its headquarters in Britain. Those countries competing to host the planned European Trade Marks Office had argued that Britain's trade mark system was so archaic that Britain could hardly be entrusted to host the headquarters office of the new European system. The government responded to such criticism by passing the service trade mark legislation which came into force in 1986 and, since that time, there has been an enormous rush by service brand owners to register service trade marks in such areas as financial services, marketing, telecommunication services, computing and so forth. Already the services classes of the UK Trade Marks Register are becoming as crowded as sectors such as pharmaceuticals and foodstuffs.

5
The use of the corporate brand

The use of branding to help create a brand personality which is differentiated, appropriate and appealing need not be applied to just soft drinks, unit trusts, hamburgers or toiletry products. An entire company can in fact be treated as a brand in the sense that a corporate brand can offer to consumers reassurance as to the consistency, quality and value of the products or services provided by the company.

Within companies branding is used by corporations in three quite different ways.

The monolithic approach

This approach is used by companies such as Sainsbury, IBM and British Telecom and is characterised by the fact that the corporate name itself is used as the primary communications tool at all levels in the company and at every point of contact which the company has with its various audiences. It may be used therefore in dealings with the stock market, on employee pension plans, in the sponsorship of civic events and on all products and services produced by the company ranging, perhaps, (in the case of IBM) from mainframe computers to widgets or (in the case of British Telecom) from communications satellites to novelty telephones.

The 'monolithic' branding approach is most commonly used when the activities of the company and the markets it serves are essentially homogeneous. (Sainsbury uses the Homebase name for its do-it-yourself retailing activities, which are also given the (albeit low key) Sainsbury corporate endorsement.) This approach is also often used when the company has developed mainly by organic growth rather than acquisition and when the company has as a result a single internal culture.

Although the use of 'monolithic' to describe such a branding policy is slightly pejorative and perhaps does less than justice to the remarkable successes of companies such as IBM, Hertz, Mercedes-Benz and Sony, it does nonetheless capture one of the features of this branding strategy – its relative inflexibility. In order to achieve greater flexibility IBM has recently started to develop sub-brands for important individual products and services. The exclusive use of the IBM corporate name as the key component in the company's brand communications has prevented the development of separate brand personalities and, it is believed, has left the company open to niche competition from competitors with more targeted brand strategies. Apple, for example, has been remarkably successful in targeting the microcomputer sector of the market and, more recently, the desk-top publishing and computer-aided design sectors. Its more user-friendly brand personality has played a significant role in its success.

The endorsed approach

The endorsed approach is one where the corporate name is used in association with product or divisional brands so that endorsement is provided to the individual product or service yet at the same time each product or service is allowed to develop its own separate personality. For example, Rowntree have, in recent years, increasingly used the Rowntree house brand as a corporate endorsement across its entire range of confectionery products (Kit-Kat by Rowntree). Ford and many other car manufacturers have always boldly endorsed their products so that their name can automatically be associated with the model: Model T Ford, Triumph Spitfire, Vauxhall Cavalier are just three examples.

The use of a corporate endorsement as a form of 'umbrella' brand lends security and value to the individual product brands and, when properly used, this approach can result in the best of all worlds for the brand owner. When United Biscuits, for example, launched their Hob-nobs brand they did so under the McVitie's umbrella brand. McVitie's is the clear market leader in biscuits in Britain and so the corporate name

47

lent the product brand enormous credibility with both the consumer and the retail trade. Much of the equity of the McVitie's brand was thus extended to the Hob-nobs brand yet, over a relatively short period of time, the Hob-nobs brand has achieved such clear differentiation that the McVitie's umbrella could probably now be withdrawn without any negative effect on the Hob-nobs brand.

The advantages of the endorsed branding route are that it allows a new brand to develop its own differentiated personality while at the same time allowing positive existing brand equities to be transferred to the new brand. The difficulties of this approach lie primarily in the area of execution. It requires skill and sureness of touch to blend harmoniously two separate brand personalities in a way that allows the development of a new brand personality without confusing or damaging the personality of the house brand.

The 'simple' approach

The term 'simple' also does less than justice to this branding approach and to the many successful companies that have applied it so skilfully. Under this system the brand is king and is used as the sole means of communicating brand values to the consumer. The corporate brand therefore plays little or no part in communications with the consumer and is used primarily for communications with specialist audiences such as investors.

This branding philosophy is followed by such leading brand owners as Mars, Procter and Gamble, and Unilever, all of whom enjoy a formidable reputation for their skills in brand management. Indeed, Mars have refined the strategy further into one of 'power branding', an approach to branding which seeks to create brands which dominate their sectors, set and maintain the benchmarks of quality, price and product specification and subordinate all other brands to the authority of the market leader.

'Simple', free-standing brands flourish in such markets as confectionery, pet foods, soft drinks and detergents where an individual brand can achieve considerable volume and can thus justify the considerable costs of launch, brand building and brand maintenance. It works less well in more fragmented markets such as mainstream human foods where consumers constantly seek new varieties and flavours and thus where umbrella brands tend to be used. Heinz, Campbell's and Crosse and

48

Blackwell all use endorsed or umbrella brands and there is a wide proliferation of different products sold under each of these brands. In such instances the cost of supporting each product variant or group of variants as a separate brand would be prohibitively expensive and endorsed branding is the only realistic strategy.)

'Simple', free-standing brands represent in some ways the 'purest' form of brand and brands of this type (for example Coca-Cola, Mars, Persil and Marmite) are those which are easiest to value, transfer and, in many respects, to manage as they are distinct, unequivocal pieces of property. They are also, however, the most difficult and expensive brands to establish and maintain, particularly in today's markets with escalating media costs and massively increased competition.

Preferred brand structures

There is no 'correct' way for a company to structure its branding activities, and even some of those companies cited as examples, in fact adopt a more hybrid approach in certain instances. McVitie's, for example, is an umbrella brand within the United Biscuits organisation and is not, therefore, also a corporate brand which is also used for other audiences, for example the City. It is also not the only umbrella used within United Biscuits as other brands such as Ross and Youngs are used in other product areas. Sainsbury, even though it primarily follows the monolithic approach (leaving aside the specialist Homebase example mentioned earlier), has started to develop closely targeted product brands under the Sainsbury endorsement; the company is therefore moving from the monolithic to the endorsed approach. Unilever is yet another example of a more complex branding structure: even though the detergent brands are primarily free-standing (and hence 'simple') brands, the Lever house brand is now used, albeit in a somewhat low-key fashion, as a form of umbrella endorsement. Thus, in this sector of its business, Unilever is starting to move from a simple to an endorsed approach.

Indeed, there is evidence of an increasing trend towards endorsed branding by companies who previously relied upon either the monolithic or the simple approach. On the one hand, companies that have traditionally used a single corporate brand on all their products and services are finding that this approach affords little opportunity for the development of closely targeted brand personalities; they are therefore increasingly seeking to develop product brands or sub-brands in close association with the main corporate brand in order to provide differentiation in their products. On the other hand, companies such as Mars and Unilever, which traditionally have used a simple branding structure whereby each brand has acted as a separate profit centre with its own advertising budget and brand management structure, are finding that the costs of continuing this policy are becoming so massive that there are benefits in 'stretching' each brand a little and thus using more effectively the equity inherent in the brand. They are therefore looking at line extensions as well as at introducing a more generalised corporate endorsement into the branding structure so that each brand will receive some corporate support even if on a year-on-year basis, it does not always receive its own substantial promotional budget. (Mars, for example, has recently introduced ice cream and a chocolate drink which bear the Mars brand name.)

The benefits of a corporate endorsement can also be exploited through licensing. Porsche, for example, gain a considerable income from licensing their name for use on products such as sunglasses and watches. Jaguar has now started to license the Jaguar name in respect of men's fragrances; and both Martini and Cinzano use their corporate names to endorse ranges of clothing.

As the value and importance of brands become increasingly recognised, and as the costs and risks of new brand development escalate, brand owners are starting to pay far more attention to the exploitation of their brand assets and are thus seeking novel ways in which to use branding to gain a competitive advantage in the marketplace. The result is that the branding landscape is becoming altogether more varied and lush, and the ways in which branding is used are becoming more complex and imaginative.

A key feature which is emerging is the increased use of corporate brands or umbrella brands. In many instances, particularly in larger companies, these umbrella brands were former corporate names which were absorbed in the past into larger groups thus becoming divisional or house brands. Examples of such brands are Sharwood, now part of Ranks Hovis McDougall, and Colman's, now part of Reckitt and Colman.

The audiences of a company

A company has a variety of audiences and it needs to communicate with all of them in an efficient and appropriate manner. At one level, the company needs to communicate its corporate brand and identity, together with its objectives and aspirations, to investors and potential investors. The message that the company wishes to communicate here is normally that it is a good investment with good prospects. In order to do this, it uses corporate advertising together with financial public relations and other investor relations techniques. The overall strength and coherence of the corporate personality and identity is of critical importance if the company is to receive the continuing support of investors, particularly when the going gets tough.

At a divisional or operating company level, the corporation also has a series of important audiences. Employees within the operating companies often identify primarily with the division for which they work rather than with the overall company, and trade relations too are often most powerfully established at this level. Again, the organisation needs a strong identity at divisional level which can act as a focus for employee and trade loyalty and which implies that the business is good both to be part of and to work with. At this level, PR activities, trade advertising and employee relations all play an important role in establishing and maintaining divisional brands.

The third level of branding is at the consumer level. Consumers are generally ill-informed and uninterested in corporate structures and aspirations. They are faced each day with hundreds, even thousands, of individual brand purchasing decisions, and it is the function of the brand to reassure the consumer at point-of-sale that the product or service in question is the best choice for his or her needs. This is done through advertising, packaging and such other communications media as public relations.

Any company, therefore, employs branding techniques at a variety of levels. Sometimes, as with IBM, the same brand name is used at all levels but the presentation and messages appropriate at each level are quite different. At other times the brands used at each level can be entirely different. For example, in the case of Unilever the brand which is used at the corporate level is the Unilever brand name; at operating level a series of quite different brands are used including Lever Brothers, Van den Berghs, Bird's Eye and Batchelor's; at the consumer level a series of separate consumer brands are used as more-or-less free-standing brands although occasionally with some divisional endorsement.

The complexity of the various possible branding structures which confront a company make it important that a clear corporate branding strategy is developed and communicated; otherwise there is obvious scope for branding anarchy. Frequently it seems that companies adopt and then discard branding structures and strategies without any firm overall policy or any consideration as to the effect that the changes may have on the loyalties of the various audiences either at consumer, divisional or corporate level. Cited earlier was the example of how Rowntree started to use a brand strategy which relied upon strong product branding but which also contained low-key corporate endorsement – all television advertisements, for example, showed the Rowntree logo at the end of the commercial. It was, however, not clear what function the corporate endorsement was meant to serve and its use appeared to many observers to be altogether half-hearted. It has been argued, perhaps with the benefit of hindsight, that the apparent failure by Rowntree to resolve fundamental branding strategy issues (as manifested by the hybrid branding policy it started to follow), lies at the heart of its failure to resist the Nestlé takeover bid. Nestlé, it is argued, were able to identify brand strengths and values which were only partially appreciated by Rowntree's own management and which, therefore, had not been adequately communicated to investors. When Nestlé launched a hostile bid based upon a clear appreciation of these underlying brand values which Rowntree management had previously failed to communicate to its investors, investors saw little reason to support the company's management and preferred instead to sell out to the predator.

It is essential, therefore, that corporations think through branding issues and determine which brands will be used at each level in the organisation and the role of each brand. Sometimes it may be desirable to devise a strategy which links all the various brands into an integrated system but which preserves the individual definition and personality of each. Lucas Industries, for example, the manufacturer of electrical and related products supplied mainly to the automotive industry, uses the Lucas brand as a corporate brand but has a variety of divisional brands including Lucas, Girling and CAV. Below these there is a host of individual product brands. This system delegates a large measure of branding autonomy below the corporate brand level, but a powerful group-wide visual identity system is used to link all the various activities into a coherent whole. Other approaches followed by organisations to provide 'local autonomy but group-wide coherence' are systems whereby individual divisions and products are largely free-standing but mention is made in all literature and on all stationery and products that 'company A is a member of the XYZ Group'.

Developing corporate brands

When developing corporate or divisional brands the same care needs to be taken as when developing consumer brands. It is very tempting for companies to assume that the audiences they are addressing are so specialised and well-informed that the choice of corporate name is of little consequence. In the computer industry, for example, the example of IBM has been so overwhelmingly strong that a number of other computer manufacturers have, perhaps subconsciously, copied IBM in choosing a corporate name. ICL of Britain is an example of a company which has, it seems, worked on the principle that 'if initials are good enough for IBM they are good enough for us' and what does it matter anyhow? In fact, the specialist audiences addressed by the company are particularly important and by no means as interested or informed as the company might like to think. It is also particularly difficult to invest sets of initials with distinctiveness and personality, and it is dangerous to overlook the fact that IBM has had decades of investment in its corporate brand in order to bring it to the position of strength that it enjoys today.

British Telecom is another company which, arguably, has set itself a more difficult task through its choice of corporate brand than it might otherwise have done. In the mid-1970s, when the telecommunication activities of the Post Office were split from the postal activities to form British Telecom, the company probably little realised that in less than a decade it would be privatised and would be expected not just to compete in its home market but around the world. When British Telecom was formed, other telecommunications monopolies in other countries were also being split off from the postal authorities and all tended to adopt purely descriptive names such as British Telecom, Australia Telecom and so forth. Simple descriptive names of this type serve reasonably well in their home markets when they enjoy a monopoly but they are much less well adapted to international use where the fact of being a British or Australian telecommunications supplier may cut little ice with customers. Indeed, it may even be a distinct disadvantage.

The choice of corporate name can, therefore, be important to a company both in marketing terms and in terms of retaining flexibility; it can also play a key role in shaping attitudes, even at the level of sophisticated investors. Woolworth Holdings found, for example, prior to changing its name to Kingfisher, that the use of the Woolworth name in the corporate title constantly focused investors' attention on the F.W. Woolworth store chain, resulting in the successful activities of B&Q, Comet and the other retailing divisions being somewhat overlooked.

Conclusions

There is no 'ideal' structure for the use of branding within a corporation. In practice, the ways in which companies have adopted branding vary enormously and are constantly changing. 3M, for example, one of the world's most successful and innovative businesses, use the 3M corporate endorsement very powerfully indeed on all products and regard the 3M name, plus powerful sub-brands such as Scotch, as being corporate assets available to all divisions with the minimum of control. The company organises itself into small specialist groups and encourages and rewards entrepreneurial activity and innovation. It sets standards as to the precise ways in which the valuable corporate brands are to be used but generally, as long as these standards are met, it is not concerned as to the products upon which they are used. The Scotch brand has, therefore, been used on a whole host of products including adhesive tapes, photographic films and fabric protectors.

Whatever system of branding is adopted clear branding rules and strategies need to be established. It must also be recognised that each of the brands, be it at a corporate, divisional or product level, has its own values and attributes which need to be clearly understood and precisely communicated. If the brand owner does not clearly understand the values and attributes inherent in each of his or her brands it is quite certain that the various target audiences will have no understanding of them either.

6
Branding industrial products

It is sometimes assumed that branding is a phenomenon confined to consumer products; that brand loyalty is a form of habitual, non-rational behaviour which applies to (mainly) soap flakes and detergents but which has no chance of survival in the more 'rational' world of 'serious' products such as electric motors, office machinery or therapeutic drugs.

The role of industrial brands

Some of the strongest brands exist in non-consumer products sectors – examples include Hibitane, an antiseptic surgical scrub from ICI, Salamander, a thermal ceramic for use in crucibles, Laserjet, a laser printer from Hewlett-Packard, and RoundUp, a herbicide from Monsanto. The reason for the strength of such brands is that brands serve exactly the same function in industrial markets as in consumer markets: they provide the consumer with a guarantee of quality, origin, value and performance; they provide a form of convenient short-hand for decision making and they help to simplify complexity. For the brand owner they provide a means of talking directly to the consumer, they serve as a focus for consumer loyalties and they act as a means of 'capturing' promotional investment. They thus become strong and enduring assets which increase in strength and value with use and help the manufacturer resist competitive attack.

Consider the role of brands in the market for office equipment. Until ten years or so ago the average investment in equipment to support one office worker was only a few hundred pounds, a tiny fraction of the invested capital for the average industrial worker. Although this situation has by no means been reversed, in the last decade massive investment has been made in office automation including computers, word processors, laser printers, monochrome and colour photocopiers, fax machines and so on. Branding has played an enormous part in helping to shape consumer purchasing decisions and attitudes. Apple has been enormously successful in this sector. In the 1950s, 1960s and much of the 1970s computers and computing were mysterious and exclusive to experts. This esotericism tended in turn to be fostered by the suppliers themselves: sales literature was full of jargon, advertising was directed at experts, and complex branding strategies were employed which allowed only those who knew largely what they wanted to shop with confidence. This branding strategy worked well enough when computers were massively expensive and the sole preserve of the expert, (though even then many company managers often felt profoundly uneasy at authorising huge expenditure on products they did not understand). In the late 1970s, however, things started to change. Computers suddenly became inexpensive and much of the specification and purchasing of computers passed to non-experts. Apple entered the scene with a branding strategy which was approachable, no-nonsense and which demystified computing. It was fresh, different and, importantly, the products themselves were innovative and of high quality. It quickly wrong-footed virtually all other computer manufacturers by making them appear remote and trapped in their own arcane rituals and language. What had once been a major benefit of the computer companies – the fact that their products and the way they were presented implied innovativeness, technology, expertise etc, – quickly turned into a hindrance as they came to be seen as hide-bound and divorced from the needs of the market.

The pharmaceutical sector

It has been suggested, following the Falklands War, that it has become a sign of national virility for countries to possess Exocet missiles and that the benefits of ownership are mainly non-tangible, relating to the brand name. But it is not just in those business or industrial sectors where non-experts make the purchasing decisions that branding has a role to play.

The pharmaceutical sector

The ethical drug industry is a persuasive example of an industry where virtually all its products are purchased by well-trained specialists supposedly able to ignore the blandishments of advertising, drug company representatives or brand name appeals and make decisions purely on the basis of rational, technical, performance factors. In fact, branding often plays an important role. Indeed, the appeal of brands can be sufficiently strong that doctors often prefer to prescribe by brand name because of the reassurance afforded them by the name. This happens in spite of policies of generic substitution in order to reduce public expenditure in countries like the United States and Britain where the government is ultimately responsible for a large proportion of all drug purchases. The advantage of generic substitutes, which are chemically identical off-patent unbranded versions of the branded product prescribed by the doctor, is that they carry none of the costs of product development, trial and back-up and are therefore invariably cheaper than their branded counterparts. A recent issue of *Drugs and Therapeutics Bulletin* a news-sheet for doctors published by the Consumers' Association but funded by the British government, estimated that wide prescribing of generic rather than branded drugs could save the National Health Service up to £100 million a year, or some 5 per cent of its pharmaceuticals bill. The bulletin considered the possibility that wider use of generic medications would lead to lower quality drugs and would increase the risks to patients but described most of the evidence on such matters as 'anecdotal'.

However, even if the harm caused to patients in the developed world by generic substitution is limited, this is not always the case. There are numerous examples of counterfeit pharmaceutical products, particularly in the Third World, and the evidence in this area is far from anecdotal. Countries such as Pakistan and Thailand have flourishing counterfeit pharmaceutical industries and it is the trade mark owners who, it appears, are most active in identifying the counterfeiters and stamping out this harmful practice, not governmental and regulatory bodies.

The reason why such counterfeiting needs to be stamped out is not just to protect the reputation of the wronged trade mark owner, but also because most such counterfeit drugs are significantly inferior and therefore potentially dangerous. (See also Chapter 14.) The widespread use of branded products protects consumer interests because their producers maintain quality and purity, keep to specifications, and resist counterfeiting and other unfair practices.

Branding raw materials

Another example of how branding can work in industrial sectors can be drawn from the plastics industry. The giant chemical companies now produce a bewildering array of different types of raw plastic and, within each type, a wide range of different grades. Just as wide is the range of processes and applications which use these products – blown film for packaging, extrusions for building products, thermoformed products for structural packaging, engineering products for the motor industry and so on.

A few plastics producers specialise in one or other type of plastic but most of the giant companies offer a more-or-less comprehensive range embracing all the major plastics materials. Huge, sophisticated international sales and marketing networks exist to service their massive customer bases. These can range from major consumers of plastic such as Mercedes-Benz which produces large structural automotive components, to small injection moulders with one or two machines producing components for telephones or heat pumps, handles for plastic carrier bags or dolls house doors.

Major producers such as Shell, BP Chemicals or Monsanto may well produce thousands of different products, supply tens of thousands of different accounts and may need to address themselves to hundreds of thousands of so-called specialists all of whom are involved in some fashion in the purchasing decision. Many of these specialists will be technicians whose approval is needed as to the type and grade of product required to do a particular job. Others will include purchasing agents who, once the need for a particular type of product is identified, will be responsible for shortlisting suitable suppliers, negotiating price, arranging delivery, agreeing contract terms and so on; university professors whose opinions as to the selection or otherwise of a particular type of plastic may be influential; equipment suppliers who may need to produce or adapt production machinery to suit a particular plastics product, and so on.

Several such specialists are likely to be involved in some way in each purchasing decision; and all will be bombarded with product information, sales literature, requests for meetings, invitations to visit trade fairs, symposia, conferences, etc. The world of the industrial 'consumer' is therefore every bit as busy and crowded in branding terms as the world of the domestic consumer. The competition for attention is fierce. Moreover, even though the industrial purchaser is essentially a 'rational' consumer, it should not be thought that the domestic consumer is 'irrational'. After all, the domestic consumer is spending his or her own money; the industrial consumer is not.

In industrial markets, branding functions in precisely the same way as in other markets by making purchasing and specification easier, by simplifying complexity and by providing reassurance. Naturally the house brand (e.g. Shell, BP, Monsanto) plays an important branding role, particularly in providing reassurance, but product branding has a major role too.

If BP, for example, were simply to use alpha-numeric codes or product descriptions to identify individual products then all the focus of branding would be directed towards the house brand. There is then a danger that any such house brand would be altogether too generalised to function, without other brand support, as the main focus of branding. In addition, the use of alpha-numeric coding systems or simple product descriptions (e.g. BP XRF39K Drainage Pipe Grade Extrudable Polypropylene) leads to a largely undifferentiated 'soup' which the specialists within the company may know and understand but which is impenetrable and off-putting to the consumer, even if he or she is relatively well-informed.

A more appropriate route, and one which BP Chemicals has in fact adopted, is to use the house brand together with separate brand names for major families of products, plus simple alpha-numeric codes to denote particular types and grades. Thus, for example, within the BP family of products Novex is the international brand name for low density polyethylene (LDPE), Innovex is used for linear low density polyethylene (LLDPE) and Rigidex for high density polyethylene (HDPE). This branding system not only introduces a certain amount of light and shade into what would otherwise be a somewhat blank branding landscape, but it also helps evolve a branding 'culture' whereby new brands, when launched, can benefit from the equity established in existing brands. Thus any new BP brand launched in the sector using the -ex suffix will initially benefit from the positive associations developed by the existing -ex family of brands.

The use of a consistent branding strategy of this type ensures that each new brand gains some leverage from the equity in the established brands. Thus new brand launches can be made more easily and cheaply and the necessary on-going brand support can be reduced. At the same time, however, each brand is able to develop its own separate and distinctive brand personality.

Industrial consumers

Industrial products, therefore, cover a very broad spectrum and include business-to-business products and services, true industrial products such as industrial raw materials and components as well as sophisticated, specialist products such as drugs and farm machinery which are sold to large, highly specialist sectors. Consumers in all these sectors, however, share a number of key features – they are mainly busy, they are unlikely to be absorbed in the precise details of the products that a supplier is trying to sell them, and they are bombarded with hundreds of different product messages from all possible directions. A doctor, for example, is probably more preoccupied with patient problems than with the details of the efficacy of a new drug; a farmer is likely to be more concerned with the intervention price for wheat being paid under the EEC Common Agricultural Policy than with whether insecticide X is marginally better, in certain applications, than insecticide Y.

Although brands in the industrial sector serve precisely the same role as brands in the consumer sector, their valuation must necessarily differ. One reason for this is that in practice, the industrial consumer is arguably easier to target and influence than the domestic consumer. Competitors can, therefore, dislodge an established industrial brand more readily and such brands are thus more vulnerable than consumer brands. A second reason is that the intangible features of the brand play a less potent role in industrial purchase decisions than in the consumer sector. For these reasons the underlying strength of the branding 'bond' is often lower in industrial sectors than in consumer sectors, and hence when valuing brands in the industrial sector it is usually necessary to apply somewhat lower multiples than can be applied in the consumer sector. (See Chapter 16 for further discussion of brand valuation.) Such factors, however, do not detract from the overwhelming arguments in favour of the adoption of branding in the industrial sector.

7
Own label

Retailing manufacturers' brands only

Retailers have developed a range of different strategies for attracting customers into their stores and for encouraging those customers to buy (and to continue to buy) the goods or services available from them rather than from competitors. One such strategy is that of selling the same branded products as are available elsewhere but to differentiate the stores in some way. Methods of store differentiation are many and include price, range, convenience and the overall shopping experience offered to customers. British retailers which adopt this strategy range from, on the one hand, Poundstretcher (focusing on a value-for-money strategy), Queensway (a chain of out-of-town furniture supermarkets which operates in a weakly branded product sector and whose strategy relies mainly upon range, delivery and convenience to distinguish itself from competitors) and, at the other end of the scale, Harrods, an exclusive department store selling all types of products from sugar to fur coats, mainly under manufacturers' brand names, and which differentiates itself through the unique 'Harrods shopping experience'. Broad retail strategies in the United States and other countries are often similar to those used in Britain.

Own label retailers

Then there are those retailers who more-or-less exclusively sell own label products – branded products which are specially produced for them under their brand name and to their specification and which are not available from any other source. In Britain the best known such retailer is Marks and Spencer, which sells under the St Michael brand name; others are MFI (in furniture), Mothercare (baby and child products) and Habitat (furniture, furnishing and housewares).

Between these two extremes (exclusively manufacturers' brands and exclusively own label) lie the majority of retailers who sell both manufacturers' brands and own brands. Sainsbury is a typical example. The Sainsbury name is well known and respected for quality and value and sits comfortably on a wide range of products, yet perhaps only half of the products on sale in a Sainsbury store are own label brands. In most product categories Sainsbury will stock the leading manufacturer brand plus one or two familiar branded alternatives. In addition, Sainsbury normally offers own label alternatives. As Sainsbury products enjoy an excellent reputation and usually offer good value for money, in some product sectors sales of the own label products will match or even exceed sales of all the manufacturer brands combined.

The growth of own label

Own label brands are, of course, a strategy which can normally be followed only by the larger retailer. Until the last war, the major own label retailer in Britain was the Co-op which often supplied the products from its own factories. In certain categories such as tea, Co-op products enjoyed a good reputation but mostly they failed to match the standards of quality and design of the manufacturers' brands. Own labels in general were often considered merely a cheap and inferior alternative to the 'real' branded products, the manufacturers' brands, an image which persisted until the late 1960s/early 1970s.

Retailers were drawn to an own label strategy mainly for financial reasons: suppliers who were able to dispense with elaborate overheads, research and development, advertising, a sales force, or who had spare production capacity, would offer retailers unbranded products at low prices. Retailers, who operate in an extremely competitive environment, were attracted to the opportunity to offer their customers cheaper products yet still maintain or even improve their margins. Faced with the choice of attaching concocted brand names to those products (which in any case would be totally unknown to customers and would never receive any promotional support) or using their house brand, they tended to prefer the own label route.

From the early 1970s onwards there has been an increasing concentration of grocery retailing in the United Kingdom into the hands of a few major groups. Small independent grocers and local family stores have been squeezed out, and groups such as Tesco, Asda, Gateway, Waitrose and Sainsbury now dominate the market. Increased mobility on the part of the consumer and a shift towards large, edge-of-town and out-of-town supermarkets and superstores demanding massive invest- ment and much more sophisticated management and controls have played a large part in this, as have the greater overall value and choice offered by such stores. The result has been an increased concentration of retail buying power as well as sharply increased competition between the major chains.

One key area in which this competition has manifested itself has been in the growth in the variety and quality of own label products, a development which in large part has been inspired by the outstanding success of the own label products of Marks and Spencer. Major retailers, who had often embarked on an own label strategy quite tentatively, began to realise that own labels could be much, much more than merely cheap alternatives to manufacturers' brands. They came to realise, too, that their buying power and their closeness to the consumer placed them in a powerful position to transform the role of own label in their stores.

Own label initiatives

One of the first initiatives which retailers took to upgrade their own label products was in the area of packaging. Previously, own label packaging endorsed the general perception of the product as a cheap alternative to manufacturers' brands. Retailers tackled the problem of drabness head on: groups such as Sainsbury, Tesco and Asda appointed design co- ordinators at a senior level who were given the tasks of improving the quality of design of all own label packaging and of instituting an own label 'look' for the entire product range.

Such initiatives have proved an unqualified success. In Britain today retailers are often the major customers of the leading package design houses, and much of the most innovative and attractive packaging design

Own label

is now initiated by retailers. Much own label packaging now owes little or nothing to manufacturers' brands and, indeed, manufacturers' brands often appear drab and pedestrian by comparison: a reversal of the previous position.

It is not just in the packaging area that own label brands have blossomed. As discussed in Chapter 3, retailers have often been far more innovative and quick to respond in the branding area than the manufacturers. Retail buyers who, previously, were responsible mainly for price and contract negotations with suppliers, for ensuring stock availability and for stock control, have increasingly been cast in a much more creative, entrepreneurial role. They have, generally, responded positively. Once they realised that they could make their own label products as interesting, or even more interesting, in visual and packaging terms than the equivalent manufacturers' brands, they started to look at other ways in which they could improve their brands, their sales and their margins. Retail buyers were transformed, in effect, into brand managers.

One obvious strategy for these newly created brand managers has been to exploit their brands further through new brand development. Retail buyers have the powerful advantage that they have immediate access to retail stores and hence are able quickly, cheaply and efficiently to put their new products in front of consumers and determine their likely success or otherwise.

Nor are they burdened by the entrenched attitudes of R&D departments, manufacturing divisions or so forth, preventing them from developing their concepts. Retail buyers have been quick to exploit the new product development opportunities provided by guaranteed shelf space, quick feedback as to consumer acceptance or otherwise, and the competition amongst suppliers to turn new product concepts into reality in the hope of large contracts if the product proves successful.

In Britain many of the most innovative food and drink products and range extensions coming onto the market are in the own label area. These include chilled and frozen meals, new snack products, environmentally sound products and 'healthy eating' products specially designed for changing lifestyles. As discussed earlier, much of the initiative in the new brand area has moved from the manufacturer to the retailer, a development which is now echoed in other parts of Europe, particularly Sweden, Switzerland and Germany. There are signs too that this trend is starting to take hold in countries such as the United States and Australia.

The retail brand

The spread of own label brands is, however, of far deeper significance than the mere fact that the retailer is starting to call the shots. What is happening is that retailers now recognise that they are, in effect, brands. Retailing is becoming far more than just trading, of setting out one's stall, buying at one price, selling at another and hoping to make a profit on the difference. Rather, retailing is becoming about building a brand identity, creating a brand personality which is differentiated, appealing and enduring. Terry Leahy, a director of Tesco, summed it up succinctly when he said:

> Retailers have now recognised that a supermarket need not be just a place to buy a selection of brands. Instead, the shop itself, its location, its atmosphere, the service it offers, the range of goods and prices, can become the brand, and retailers can begin to extract the benefits which investment in branding can bring. The value which the store name acquires can be transferred to a range of goods which themselves reinforce the image of the store.

The adoption of branding techniques by retailers will have a powerful influence on brand owners, not just in grocery sectors but across the board. Generally retailers are neutral towards brand owners; they have no wish to destroy manufacturers' brands and are by no means antagonistic towards such brands. Nonetheless, they will not support manufacturers' brands unless there is some benefit to themselves in doing so. Most major retailers now adopt a 'mixed' branding policy: they stock those manufacturers' brands which are liked and respected by consumers and which are well-priced and supported by their owners. They also ensure that they have well-priced, well-packed own label products in all key product sectors. Clearly if manufacturers' brands do not maintain their appeal to consumers then retailers will discontinue their support and will shift emphasis increasingly towards own label brands.

Own label and small retailers

In order to pursue, through the use of own label products, a strong retail branding strategy, retailers need considerable purchasing power. They need also to be quite sophisticated so as to be able to specify, source and

65

Own label

test own label products. This strategy has not, therefore, been one that small retailers have been able readily to follow, and manufacturers' brands have thus been able to maintain their hold in this area. Even here, however, the situation is changing. When retailing first started to evolve from small-scale, fragmented owner-managed stores into today's large, integrated retailing chains, the small stores fought back – or tried to do so – by forming buying consortia to aggregate their purchasing power so as to match that of the larger chains. Thus organisations such as Spar and Mace were born. The success of such consortia has been only partial but they have nonetheless helped the small, independent units to survive in an increasingly competitive environment. These buying consortia are now starting to parallel the own label developments of the major retailers by developing 'own label' products for sale by small, independent retailers.

Implications for manufacturers

It is easy to suggest that the growth of own label brands over the last twenty years heralds the demise of conventional manufacturers' brands, that branding is now evolving into a new and quite different phenomenon. In fact, the adoption of branding techniques and concepts by retailers serves mainly to demonstrate the robustness and adaptability of the branding concept rather than its demise.

What is perhaps more surprising than the fact that retailers are adopting branding techniques is the relative lack of response to this development by manufacturers. When own label products were first introduced on a wide scale in the 1960s and 1970s branded goods manufacturers were not unduly worried as the products were clearly inferior and appealed to consumers largely on price. Weak brands with little consumer recognition and appeal and which themselves survived mainly on price were most seriously affected; leading brands were affected hardly at all. During the last ten to fifteen years, as own label brands have started to appeal on grounds other than price, brand leaders have become much more concerned about the own label phenomenon but have gained comfort from the fact that in recent years own label penetration appears to have levelled off. In addition, many leading brand owners such as United Biscuits and Ranks Hovis McDougall have established substantial businesses servicing the own label requirements of retailers.

66

Implications for manufacturers

However, the major threat to manufacturers' brands stems not from any desire on the part of the retailer to destroy the power of the manufacturer or from any instinct which leads the retailer to put his name on everything he sells but, rather, from the fact that retailers often seem genuinely to be the more innovative and responsive to consumer needs. In other words, the major threat to manufacturers arises from the fact that own label brands are often better than the branded products of the manufacturers.

Retailers are well aware that they rely upon efficient and innovative suppliers for the products they sell. Most retailers view the notion of their entering manufacturing with something approaching horror. They are, therefore, not out to destroy the manufacturer and most retailers welcome the notion of a number of vigorous, successful suppliers competing for their business. But they do, quite clearly, like to control the manufacturer; they like to set prices, impose delivery and other conditions, and generally subordinate the manufacturer to their will. Retailers are, after all, the customers in this instance.

The most potent weapon that the manufacturer possesses to resist the domination of the retailers and achieve a balanced, mutually productive and profitable relationship is his or her brands. If consumers demand a certain brand, and if the range of products offered by the retailer is incomplete without that brand, the retailer is obliged to do business with the brand owner. The best price, the best delivery, the most advantageous payment terms and the greatest contribution towards joint advertising will still be sought but, at the end of the day, business will be done. The brand, therefore, allows the manufacturer to 'reach over the shoulder of the retailer' (as H. G. Wells described it) direct to the consumer, and it makes for a balanced and mutually productive relationship. Own label brands only start seriously to threaten manufacturers' brands when consumers genuinely come to recognise them as being as good as manufacturers' brands, but cheaper. The threat becomes even more worrying when the consumer starts to prefer the own label brands.

There is increasing evidence in Britain that this is now happening in such sectors as grocery products and home furnishings. In these sectors own label products are starting to become the products of choice of consumers: Marks and Spencer prepared meals are widely considered to be superior to those of most manufacturers, and Laura Ashley and

Habitat have established their own label brands so powerfully that they now dominate those of manufacturers. In evolutionary terms, therefore, own label brands are starting to demonstrate that they are better adapted to the needs of consumers. They will therefore continue to flourish at the expense of existing brands and hence are by no means a short-lived phenomenon.

In many respects the own label 'threat' to existing brands closely parallels the Japanese car threat to indigenous car producers. Japanese cars first entered Western markets because they were cheap. Now, however, they are frequently more expensive than indigenous products yet are preferred by consumers for their greater sophistication, specification and reliability. Soon Japanese manufacturers will supply over half of the world's cars. In order to survive at all, European and American manufacturers have had to become more efficient and improve product quality; they have also been forced to innovate much more and to introduce new models at ever shorter intervals.

Brand owners need similarly to become much more active if they are to meet the 'threat' from own label. Product range and quality will need to be improved and in many areas new product development activity will need to be stepped up. Most importantly, the responsiveness of manufacturers to the needs of the consumer requires improvement. Thus tedious, over-elaborate market research procedures will need to be short-circuited and 'fast-focus' procedures adopted for product development, testing and launch.

Responding to own label

Achieving greater responsiveness will not be easy. One of the strengths of the retailer is that his brand inevitably has a broadly based personality and positioning. Harrods, for example, has powerful attributes of quality and sophistication, all in a relatively generalised 'British' context. The Harrods brand is not particularised to toys or food or clothing, and the brand can, therefore, be applied with more-or-less equal ease to a bottle of Scotch whisky as to an expensive fur coat. As long as certain qualities and values are preserved it is unlikely that the brand will suffer however it is used.

This is not normally true of manufacturers' brands. Generally such brands have a much more targeted positioning and part of the reason that manufacturers appear frequently much more leaden-footed than retailers in brand development activities is that much more care needs to be taken with manufacturers' brands to ensure that any development enhances the brand's appeal.

What is needed, therefore, to accompany more active and aggressive brand management is more skilful and sensitive brand management. If brand owners simply respond to own label brands by adopting a policy of pell-mell introduction of new packaging, new product variants and new line extensions, the result is likely to be brand anarchy and, ultimately, a destruction of the brand. Rather, what is required is careful brand management built upon an acute understanding of the personality of the brand, of the market that the brand serves and of consumer needs and expectations.

At present one of the key reasons for the laborious testing and research procedures that brand owners insist on prior to any changes to their brands (and to which retailers, with their own label brands, need pay much less regard) is to provide checks against ill-advised and inappropriate brand modifications. Detailed procedures for research and validation provide an opportunity for reflection and management intervention, even if they produce little data of any value to the decision-making process. Existing procedures often ensure, therefore, that the brand is not seriously weakened by ill-advised initiatives even though, at the same time, they often ensure too that the brand is not modified and developed to suit changing conditions. One of the key challenges for brand management is that of reconciling these apparently conflicting aims such that the integrity of the brand is maintained yet, at the same time, it is adapted to suit changing conditions.

8

Developing new brand names

The brand name is central to the personality of the brand, it is the main component of the brand in which the brand owner can secure legal protection and it is also the one aspect of the brand which normally never changes. It is, therefore, of vital importance to the personality of the brand and it also performs a series of key roles. Firstly, it identifies the product or service thereby allowing the consumer readily to identify, specify or even reject the brand. Secondly, it normally communicates messages to the consumer; it can do this through the descriptive content of the name, or through the associations that the brand name has acquired over time. Thirdly, it functions as a piece of legal property in which the brand owner can safely invest and which protects the interests of the brand owner from competitive trespass. The brand name therefore 'captures' the promotional investment placed in the brand and, through time and use, becomes a valuable asset: one which can be bought and sold, licensed or even mortgaged.

The brand name is, therefore, quite complex; it has both a communications role and a legal role, and it is the element of the brand which is least susceptible to change.

'Traditional' brand name development

In light of the important function that brand names perform, it is surprising how little attention has at times been given to their creation for new products or services. Normally the new product is considered and researched in depth, considerable attention is given to the pack design, to launch advertising, to media selection and to distribution arrangements yet the brand name, a central element in the personality of the brand and the one feature of the brand which never changes and upon which the company secures all its legal protection, may well be thought up by the chairman in the bath and will probably receive virtually no specialist attention. Paradoxically, the reason for this is that naming something is so 'important' that it has to be done at the top. Naming involves a form of parenthood, and who better to perform this function than the chairman?

Unfortunately, the cost to a company of making a wrong choice of brand name can be high. For example, a new and innovative product may be given a brand name which is familiar, perhaps even banal, and the product's innovative nature may well be concealed behind the bland brand name. Another common problem is that a brand name may be selected which is suitable for the home market but which turns out later to be unsuitable in overseas markets, with the result that other brand names have to be selected for those markets, causing fragmentation of brand coherence and diseconomies in the areas of production, distribution and promotion.

Another common occurrence is for a company to set its heart on a brand name which may well have profound legal problems either at home or overseas and to proceed to use the brand name in spite of the inevitable consequences. Sometimes, by restricting the specification of goods on the trade mark application or by buying off the owners of the most problematical existing trade marks, the more immediate problems in the home market can be circumvented and the brand owner is thus encouraged to go ahead with the chosen brand name. However as the brand is rolled out from one country to another the underlying problems in other jurisdictions become all too apparent and eventually, after much anguish and expense, force the adoption of another brand name for those markets.

At other times, the problems inherent in a haphazard approach to brand name development are rather more subtle. For example, at the time of launch a particular feature or attribute of the new product might be considered so overwhelmingly important that a brand name is chosen which focuses more-or-less exclusively on this attribute. Over time, however, the attribute may become of much less significance yet the focus and positioning of the brand may be forever directed towards it as it had been so unequivocally built into the brand personality through the brand name. Yet another problem arises if a brand owner adopts a name for his new product or service which is obvious and easy to imitate (for example, Innotel for an innovative telecommunications service). Even if an obvious name of this type were to prove legally available on an international basis (which is most unlikely), it may well not be sensible to adopt such a name as it may be all too easily imitated by competitors and the innovative brand may thus be swamped by a host of derivative brands all focusing on a few familiar prefixes and suffixes.

What then are the key factors to consider in the development of new brand names?

Key factors

The first key factor to consider is the degree of innovativeness or otherwise of the new product or service. If the new brand is clearly differentiated from competitive products there is little point in giving the brand a familiar name which conceals its innovativeness from the consumer. This is not to say, of course, that it is sensible to go to the other extreme and adopt for innovative products wild or bizarre brand names, though such brand names do have their place in certain product sectors (Opium and Poison have proved outstanding brand names for dramatic new fragrances; Um Bongo is a name which is memorable and fun for a fruit-based drink for children). Rather, brand owners with an innovative and differentiated new brand should seek a brand name which is differentiated from the existing culture of branding within the sector but which stops short of being eccentric or shocking.

Paradoxically, it is also frequently sensible to seek differentiation and innovation through the brand name when the brand itself is, in fact, little differentiated from the competitors'. One of the problems facing brand owners in today's highly competitive markets is that in most markets all products are produced to an extremely high standard and under tight price constraints. In many sectors the opportunity for real product innovation is strictly limited. In the lager beer market, for example, a brewer wishing to enter this sector of the British beer market with a 'mainstream' new brand is faced with extreme limitations as to what can be done as far as the product, the physical packaging, the pricing or the general look are concerned. The product has to meet certain taste

72

requirements if it is to be a mainstream beer; it must fall within a fairly closely specified price band and it probably has to be made available to consumers in bottles, cans or on draught. The opportunities for dramatic product innovation are quite limited. The market would probably not accept blue beer or pink beer or beer which costs five times more than existing beers; nor would it be appropriate to adopt radical new packaging techniques even though new bottle shapes and closure systems have their place. In practice, with many new products and services the differences between one new product or service and another must inevitably be extremely subtle, even slight, and the brand name and the packaging design and the different images and associations which these convey may be a key means of differentiation.

There are compelling reasons therefore for seeking differentiated, though by no means bizarre, brand names. On the one hand, when the product is innovative and differentiated such brand names ensure that the unique qualities and attributes of the product are not hidden behind an unimaginative brand name. On the other hand, if the new product is much like everyone else's, a differentiated brand name provides an opportunity to help it stand out in the crowd.

As discussed earlier, a further important factor which needs to be considered in the choice of a brand name is whether or not the brand is likely to become an international brand. It can be extremely easy, when developing a new brand, to disregard the international potential for the brand. This is particularly true in the case of American companies as the American market represents in many categories around 50 per cent of the world potential – why, therefore, bother about everyone else? However, the international suitability and availability of the brand name is the one aspect of the product which cannot be overlooked at the outset if the product is to have any chance of international application under the same brand name at a later date. Indeed, the coming together of consumer tastes and expectations, increased media overlaps, enlarged trading groups such as the European Community, and increased market segmentation all indicate a definite need for international branding.

Another factor which needs to be considered when choosing a brand name is the precise way in which that name will be used. If, for example, it is intended that a series of line extensions will be developed off the initial brand at a later date, it is sensible to select a name which can comfortably embrace all these extensions. Thus a name which focuses too precisely on the unique attributes of the initial product will be inappropriate. Alternatively, it may be sensible where there is likely to be a proliferation of products, to develop 'families' of brands so that all new brands can slot into an established brand naming system. Each then can develop its own brand personality but can capitalise on the qualities and equities already established in the existing brands.

Finally, it is difficult to over-emphasize the importance of the legal protection aspects of the brand name. In Britain and other common law countries where registration is not essential, it is all too easy to adopt a *laissez-faire* attitude to trade mark law and to view it as a minor irritation to be looked after by the legal department or by some remote trade mark specialist. Registered trade marks are, however, valuable and potent pieces of property with a potentially infinite life. It is essential to select a trade mark for your new product which is legally strong and which, if your product has any potential for international use, is capable of international protection. It is almost certain that if you launch a new product whose brand name has profound deficiencies you will not be able readily to repair these deficiences at a later date.

Developing a naming strategy

The first task in developing a new brand name is to crystallise out a clear product naming strategy which focuses on the product itself, the market in which the new product will operate, the objectives of the brand and the legal requirements of the brand. Figure 8.1 shows the brand name development process in diagrammatic form.

The product information you should set out includes the product concept, the satisfactions delivered by the product, the ways in which the product is differentiated from others, competition, distribution plans, plans for line extensions, the personality of the product, the use of any umbrella or house brand, the relationship, if any, of the new brand to any existing company brands and so forth.

Consideration also needs to be given to the personality of the brand, its sex (male, female, neither), whether or not the brand is to be perceived as having a specific nationality, its innovativeness and, of course, its internationality. Consideration also needs to be given as to how the brand name will be used. If, for example, the brand name will almost never be spoken, it may be possible to select a name with particularly strong visual

74

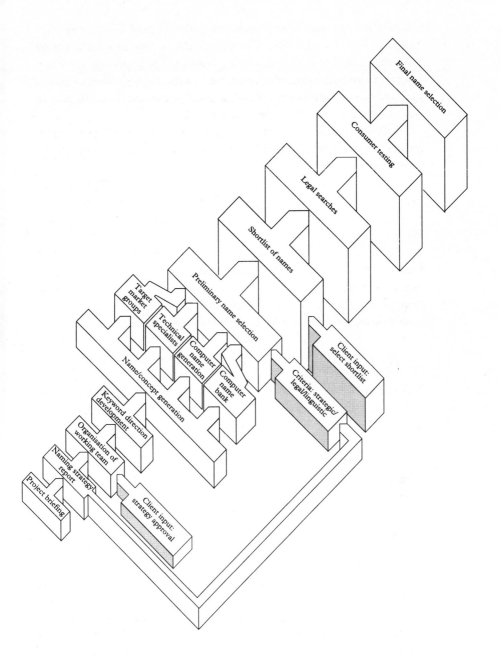

Figure 8.1 The brand name creation process

qualities but which may be less readily pronounceable. If, on the other hand, the brand has to be specified by name, for example in a bar or restaurant, the brand name must be easily pronounceable without any danger of confusion or embarrassment. It may also be sensible in such circumstances to select a brand name which is not readily corrupted or fooled around with.

Finally, all these factors need to be drawn together into a clearly enunciated and agreed brand naming strategy so that all involved in the new brand development project – the brand manager, pack designer, trade mark lawyer, advertising agency and naming consultancy – can agree on clear, unequivocal objectives for the naming exercise.

Developing naming themes

Having agreed a naming strategy the next task is to explore various naming themes. If one were naming, say, a new Japanese high performance sports car which was intended for sale in world markets a name could be developed which alludes to its country of origin (Japanese technology is now highly regarded yet overtly Japanese names have not been widely used in product branding); masculine, strong names related to international style and sophistication; names related to speed, power and performance; names related to high technology; and names related to more abstract themes such as wild animals or winds or celestial bodies, all of which have appropriate imagery and international appeal. Whichever one of these is selected will have a profound influence on the personality of the brand and the entire communications programme.

Each of the various themes will also have a quite separate degree of risk. For example, the Japanese route could, if successful, produce an outstandingly powerful and distinctive brand personality (Katana, for example, the Japanese name for an ultra high precision samurai sword has worked well in the United States on a high performance Japanese motorbike). The risks, however, of this route are relatively high as it is a new one in so far as sports cars are concerned. It may not in practice be sensible to adopt such a high-risk branding strategy, even if it promises a higher than average reward. Some of the other naming routes, on the other hand, may simply be over-worked. The theme of powerful animals, for example, has already been used successfully by scores of automotive companies and such names as Cobra, Jaguar, Mustang and

76

Panther are already in use on motor vehicles. It would seem that few reasonably familiar, appropriate and attractive names of this type are still available on an international basis.

By a process of elimination it is possible to consider, reject and prioritise creative themes and thus develop a tighter naming brief; at this stage, however, it is not necessary to be too emphatic. The next stage in the development process is to use carefully selected and managed creative or focus groups to explore specific naming themes. Members of such groups need to be selected for their creativity, language skills and ability to work as part of a team.

Such creative groups are not only expected to come up with potential names but can also be extremely useful in validating or rejecting selected naming themes. Another Japanese motor manufacturer recently used a naming consultancy to develop international brand names for a new executive motor car. The type of names that the client preferred were names associated with prestige and authority such as Senator, Crown, Ambassador and President. Many such names were already in use, apparently successfully, and the company felt sure that this was the most sensible route to follow in developing new names. A worldwide series of creative groups focusing on this theme and using target market male motorists reported, however, that although such names were not rejected out of hand they were considered rather too staid for the relatively young, successful business man or woman who drove executive cars. More interest was expressed in 'lifestyle' names, or the sorts of name that an international fragrance house might adopt for an up-market male fragrance rather than in a name like Crown or President. This response, which was more-or-less consistent internationally, led the car manufacturer to reject the original theme and focus instead on themes much more related to international sophistication and lifestyle.

Despite the usefulness of creative groups in developing names and testing and evaluating creative themes, their output often needs to be considerably supplemented by the work of copywriters, desk researchers and, in certain instances, by computer name generation techniques. These all supply additional data and facts relevant to the chosen theme, thus broadening the basis for choice of name and further fuelling the imagination.

Similarly, when developing pharmaceutical brand names, groups of doctors may be extremely useful for suggesting creative themes and certain preferred suffixes and prefixes may appear time and again. Computer name generation techniques may, however, prove much more productive than creative groups for exploring all the various word root combinations. Indeed, in such instances the computer comes into its own.

Name selection

Having developed hundreds, even thousands, of potential brand names according to a clear strategy and carefully selected creative themes, the next task is one of selection. Generally, quantity aids quality and it is sensible to first conduct a coarse screening of all the names against the agreed strategy and then, in the case of an international project, to conduct a further initial language screening of perhaps 200–300 shortlisted names. When a shortlist of this size is screened in, say, French, German, Italian, Spanish, English and Japanese it would be likely that no more than fifty or so names will prove acceptable in all these languages. Preliminary legal searches can then be undertaken at low cost on all these names. From a list of names that have survived the first legal hurdle, perhaps twenty would then be selected for detailed language checks and full international legal searches. (It often happens too that in the process of considering potential names many of the strategic issues crystallise out and the product itself starts to acquire real form and a distinct personality.)

The twenty or so shortlisted names need to be tested for linguistic suitability, pronounceability, associations and, of course, legal availability. This process is necessarily intricate and detailed and it is wise not to cut corners. A great deal of raw material needs to be fed into the naming hopper before that valuable and highly refined product is developed: the strong, appropriate and protectable brand name.

The international legal searching of potential brand names can be both extensive and costly; it also requires skill on the part of the trade mark lawyer handling the searches. The cost of searching a single trade mark in one country may well be between £300 and £500 as local attorneys must be engaged who understand the intricacies of local trade mark law and who understand, too, precisely how the name would be pronounced in their language, in order to identify those marks which might be considered to be confusingly similar. Such attorneys will conduct a search, identify potentially conflicting marks and render an opinion as to availability.

When one is searching, say, twenty marks in ten different countries the costs of the legal searching programme can mount alarmingly, as can the complexity. It is therefore sensible to undertake the searches on a sequential basis: all the marks would be searched in the first country, the survivors only in the next country, and so on. In practice, however, much can be done to remove apparent obstacles in the path of a preferred trade mark and thus to reduce the rate of attrition in the searches. Owners of apparently conflicting marks can, for example, be approached for consents, or commercial deals can be struck to clear the way. Such arrangements, however, often take many months to conclude.

A final procedure normally followed before a brand name is selected is detailed testing. Testing potential brand names for products or services which do not currently exist is exceptionally difficult and there is a real danger that consumers will attribute the highest scores in a research situation to familiar-sounding brand names and reject those that are more innovative. (It has been argued that if Steve Jobs had used conventional brand name testing techniques Apple Computer would have been called IRG Corporation or Compumax or some similarly unexciting name. Also, that if Revlon had researched Charlie it would have rejected this great name in favour of a name like Fleurs de Paris or Arc de Triomphe.)

Wherever possible a carefully simulated marketing mix test should be carried out prior to choosing the final brand name. In these tests it is important to remember that 'consumers' buy brands, not products, and that a brand is a successful blend of a variety of appeals: the product itself, the brand name, the packaging, the price and the promotion. To test brand names successfully they must, therefore, be placed in the context of the overall brand and not examined in isolation. Consumers, in order to understand and evaluate a proposed brand name, require to understand the rationale for the brand and how the brand will be used in the marketplace. Thus proper stimulus materials are needed such as comprehensive three-dimensional packs together with proposition boards or animatics that look like real advertisements. The new product concept and the new brand name need to be portrayed as clearly and realistically as possible. The more help you are able to give consumers in understanding your brand, the better placed they will be to provide you with an informed assessment of your brand name ideas.

It is not just how you present your brand name ideas to consumers which is important, though, it is also how you interpret the results. Consumers have great difficulty in spontaneously fitting new name ideas within their existing frame of reference and they tend therefore to prefer the familiar – even the banal – and to reject more innovative names. They prefer too to favour descriptive names as these are more readily understood. They also like to criticise and to show how smart they are by offering spurious objections: 'Malibu is in California and does not have coconut palms so it is no good for a coconut flavoured drink'; 'I think it is crazy to name a computer after a fruit'. Objections of this sort should normally not be taken at their face value.

At the end of the day, developing new brands is essentially a creative process with a strong legal component. Good research can certainly help, but only up to a point. Good branding is often about thinking ahead of the consumer, shaping his or her needs and desires and presenting propositions to the consumer which, with familiarity and exposure, become attractive and desirable but which initially the consumer may not respond to in a positive fashion. In the final analysis the marketing professional must exercise his or her own judgement based on familiarity with the market, intuition, input from the consumer, assistance from trade mark professionals, and a real determination to create a well-differentiated brand property.

The 'spectrum' of brand names

Brand names cover a wide spectrum from, on the one hand, totally descriptive names such as Bitter Lemon or Sava-Centre to, on the other, completely free-standing, coined names such as Kodak or Exxon. In the middle there lie associative names such as Slalom for razors (associations with twin-blade shaving) and Visa for credit cards (associations with travel and freedom) (see Figure 8.2).

Highly descriptive brand names are often favoured by advertising agencies as they communicate very directly and, it is argued, make the communications task easy. They are, however, extremely difficult to protect, they often fail to cross language barriers readily and they frequently fail to possess the texture and interest of more creative names – they can often appear rather one-dimensional and boring. Completely arbitrary, coined names, on the other hand, are potentially the strongest form of trade mark in legal terms and are afforded considerable deference

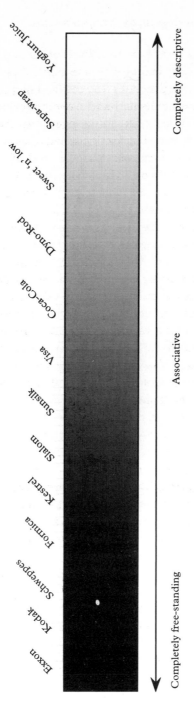

Figure 8.2 The brand name 'spectrum'

by trade mark legal systems. However, because they are completely made up they have no initial associations and considerable expenditure and effort is needed to invest the name with all the required attributes and associations. It should be said, however, that once such attributes and associations have been established, the coined brand name becomes an exceptionally powerful and unequivocal brand property as the brand owner has complete control over all the brand associations. Thus Kodak unequivocally means what Eastman Kodak requires it to mean; the Kodak brand relies upon no other associations or suggestions and embodies only those attributes imparted to it by its owners.

Generally, companies would be unwise to adopt for a new product a completely descriptive name as such names are non-distinctive and impossible to protect. On the other hand, adopting completely coined names necessitates the expenditure of substantial investment over an extended period; Kodak is now over one hundred years old. The most appropriate route for the majority of brand owners is the selection of brand names which are associative or suggestive of the product or service but which are both far from descriptive and far from totally abstract. Schweppes, for example, is in many ways an abstract name yet is fortunate to have a built-in onomatopoeia which conveys images of a fizzy effervescent drink. Sunsilk has a degree of descriptive quality yet it has, at the same time, attractive associations with the outdoors. Replay, an erasable ballpoint pen from Papermate, alludes to the nature of the pen in a way that is familiar across Europe due to the use of action replays on television.

Capturing appropriate and attractive associations in a brand name is difficult, particularly when the brand name is intended for international use. The job of the brand name is, however, critical in positioning the brand and brand owners need to be aware of the commercial and legal realities of their brand names. It takes time and money to develop strong international brand names but the investment is often well worth making.

9
Developing logos and packaging

All brands, whether they are product brands, 'umbrella' brands or corporate brands, are a synthesis of various elements, and while the brand name is frequently at the core of the brand's personality, the key visual elements used in establishing and communicating a brand's personality are the logo, the packaging and the general look of the brand.

Early use of logos

Logos have been used since the earliest times to indicate origin, ownership or association. The Austro-Hungarian Empire used the Hapsburg Eagle, and the Japanese Court the Imperial Chrysanthemum to indicate to their subjects their power and majesty. Pilgrims from all over the known world who travelled to the shrine of St James at Compostella in Spain used to carry a cockleshell to signify their devotion and piety. The Christian cross itself is a simple, powerful and emotive symbol, and perhaps the most widely used logo in human history. Logos are still used widely by non-trading bodies as well as by commercial organisations. The Royal Air Force roundel is a distinctive and familiar logo, as is the Nazi swastika, and all sorts of public and private bodies continue to use logos in order to prompt instant recognition as well as to signal ownership or origin.

Commercial organisations use logos for exactly the same reasons; they identify the organisation and its goods or services, they differentiate the organisation and its products or services from those of others, and they help develop recognition and loyalty.

The importance of consistency in the development of brand recognition and the difficulties involved in establishing a bond between the brand and the consumer were discussed earlier. Consistency is equally important in the area of logos, packaging and corporate identity. It takes long and repeated exposure to develop 'visual equity'; logos must be considered as long-term assets and should not be subject to frequent revision and alteration.

Types of logo

There are many different types of logo in commercial use ranging from corporate names or trade marks (i.e. word marks) written in a distinctive form to entirely abstract logos which are quite unrelated to the word mark or corporate name and which may have only a tenuous relationship with the activities of the corporation. Examples of logos consisting of the name written in a distinctive way include Coca-Cola, Dunhill, Pirelli, Mars and Kit-Kat. In all these instances the word mark is the main element of communication and the distinctive visual form in which the word mark is presented serves further to differentiate it. None of these brands has a logo which is separate from the name; wherever the brand name appears it does so either in a neutral type face or in its own distinctive face. This distinctive typeface is, however, intimately associated with the brand name.

Although the logo style used in conjunction with the name is, in the above instances, subordinate to the name itself, it can become a valuable and distinctive property in its own right. It would be easy to imagine, for example, a totally new brand name, perhaps Carlton-Cola, being written in the distinctive Coca-Cola typeface using the distinctive Coca-Cola red. The visual elements of the Coca-Cola name have become so familiar to us that even if another brand name is substituted we still recognise the logo and might well be confused by the substitution. For this reason companies such as Coca-Cola and Mars are just as assiduous in protecting their logos and look as they are in protecting their word marks.

At the other end of the spectrum from word marks shown in a special form are entirely abstract logos which exist quite separately from the corporate or product name (although they may indeed have some deep, core meaning to their creators). Examples include the Mercedes star, the triangular device of the National Westminster Bank and the logo based upon a sine wave used by Philips. Generally, abstract logos of this type are employed where the use of the corporate name in its full form might be problematical. The name 'National Westminster Bank', for example, is long and rather cumbersome and the triangular logo can be used instead with considerable ease and flexibility to identify the bank on cheque books, literature, signage, even on napkins and promotional items. The logo is sometimes used in close association with the corporate name, at other times it is treated as a completely free-standing visual device.

Another reason why corporations adopt separate logos is because the range of products or services offered by the business is so wide that to use the corporate name in its entirety in all instances would be extending the usage of the name too widely. British Telecom, for example, uses a separate logo consisting of a T in a circle to identify various products and services offered by the company. This is used on telephones, on manhole covers, vehicles, in advertising, etc. Logos which identify origin or ownership unequivocally and in a convenient shorthand form provide their owners with flexibility and, through constant repetition, the logo acquires visual meaning, reinforces the corporate or product name and becomes an asset in its own right.

Between the two extremes of word marks rendered in a distinctive typographic form and entirely abstract logos lies a wide variety of associative logos. Such logos are visual devices divorced from the corporate name but with a close and obvious association with the name or with the activities of the business.

Many companies use as a separate logo the first letter of the company name presented in a distinctive form (Quotient, a leading British computer software company does this). In other instances a play may be made on the corporate name: Rover, for example, uses a logo based on the prow of a Viking ship as the Vikings were sea rovers; Volkswagen use a logo incorporating a wolf's head as the home town of the Volkswagen group is Wolfsburg in West Germany; Lancia uses the lance in its corporate logo, a visual pun on its name. At other times logos may be based on the activities of the company; P&O, now a diversified company but formerly the Peninsular and Orient Steamship Line, uses a pennant or flag device which harks back to the company's origins in the shipping business; Taylor Woodrow, a major building and civil engineering construction company, uses a device of men pulling together on a rope, a striking visual symbol which suggests teamwork.

Separate logos are not usually used in association with product brands; in this area it is much more usual simply to use the word mark in a distinctive visual form. However, as the communications task becomes more complex, particularly in the case of diversified corporations or where the company possesses an unwieldy corporate name, separate logos are far more common.

The first issue to address, therefore, when developing logos and packaging is whether a separate logo is required or whether the brand name should simply be presented in a distinctive typographic fashion. In practice, the latter approach is normally the preferred solution.

Attitudes of designers

When designing logos and packaging it is often tempting for designers to regard themselves as being somehow in the business of producing art for industry. Designers sometimes prefer to see themselves as performing exclusively a creative role which owes little to the more practical constraints of business. However, to be a successful designer the designer of logos or packaging must consider and integrate important practical, strategic and creative elements.

The practical aspects to be considered in designing logos are such issues as the nature of the business or product under consideration; the range of applications upon which the new logo will be used; the countries in which it will be seen and the degree of control which the brand owner will be able to exert over the use of the logo by employees, subsidiaries, agents and others; the amount of money that the client will be prepared to spend on printing and reproduction; the extent to which a separate free-standing logo is required or whether the existing brand or corporate name can simply be used in a distinctive form, and so forth. A few examples of how these types of consideration can affect the logo design are looked at below.

1.   If a new logo is being developed for a charity which has extremely limited funds and which spends these funds carefully there is little point in the designer suggesting a solution which is expensive to implement. Even though the design might be considered attractive

by the client, it is almost certain that, over time, it will be corrupted as the charity is unlikely to continue paying for expensive printing. In such an instance, elaborate or complex logo designs which are expensive to reproduce would be inappropriate and unwise.

2. If the client is a cement company and uses its logo on everything from the chairman's notepaper to bags of cement, a design solution should be sought which is sufficiently robust to retain its distinctiveness on bags of cement yet still looks appropriate on corporate stationery and literature.

3. If a logo is being designed to accompany a festival or event which will not be repeated it may be appropriate to adopt an entirely contemporary and fashionable design. If, on the other hand, the new logo will be used for an extended period a more timeless approach will be needed; no-one wants a logo which is quite clearly frozen at a particular point in time.

4. If the client is an international corporation with sales and distribution companies around the world, the designer should be aware that the new logo will need to be reproduced very widely, often in countries without the printing technology or close controls which exist in developed countries. Logos which rely on special printing techniques, special inks or high levels of printing sophistication may be inappropriate.

Besides the practical, common sense aspects of logo design the creator of new logos must also carefully consider the strategic aspects of logos.

5. The client is a computer software company based in the United Kingdom. The company has received considerable government support to become established and counts government departments among its major clients. It is keen, therefore, to project an air of British establishment and solidity through its logo. On the other hand, it has plans to extend into Europe and the United States where such an approach might be considered less appropriate. The logo designer should be aware not just of the company's current market position but also of its long-term plans and aspirations so that the design solution which is developed can serve the company through into the medium and longer term.

6. The client is a house builder; he has a strong preference for a logo design with a building theme (your client has tentative plans to

Developing logos and packaging

expand into other forms of building). The choice is to work around a generalised building theme or to focus specifically on house building (the sole activity at present). The latter strategy may quickly become out of date if the company becomes involved in the construction of commercial or light industrial buildings. A more generalised theme relating to building is likely to be much more timeless.

7. The client has a memorable name which can be used in its entirety in all applications. Under such circumstances there may be no point in developing a separate logo as the corporate name might benefit from frequent exposure, perhaps in a distinctive typographic form, whereas the use of a separate logo might simply confuse the communications task and present the client with two communications jobs rather than one.

The designer of logos should, therefore, be in some measure a business consultant. He or she needs to be thoroughly familiar with the client's business, business plans and the practical aspects of usage and reproduction of the logo. To do this the designer should visit production locations and retail outlets, examine the client's products, talk to customers and staff, consider closely the competitive environment and what competitors are doing.

This process of internal consensus development is particularly important – just as names have a powerful emotional charge so too do logos and other visual devices, and it is likely that opinions as to the choice of logo will vary widely. The designer needs to consider all these views and develop a solution which meets the objectives of the client, which considers business realities and which also takes account of the views of all interested groups within the company.

Designing the logo

Generally, any creative solution must be rooted in thorough analysis and a clear understanding of practical problems. Nonetheless, the talented designer makes a creative leap by integrating all these factors together in a unique and distinctive fashion. Experienced logo designers know full well that the process of arriving at appropriate creative solutions is not a 'eureka' one. They need to explore dozens, even hundreds, of design approaches and gradually hone down the options into a few alternatives, all of which appear capable of performing the task in hand.

The people who will have to live with the final design are the client, and his or her staff and customers. It is important, therefore, that the designer presents a range of design solutions, explains and justifies them in detail and works closely with the client so as to benefit from the client's particular insights and experience. The creative process should, therefore, be an interactive one where various solutions are explored, refined, discussed and reworked. This process ensures not only that an appropriate, workable solution is developed but also that it is internalised and accepted within the organisation.

The most successful logos have a timeless simplicity and elegance. But creativity in the area of logos involves reconciling conflicting and complex requirements in a novel but appropriate fashion. It is all too easy to come up with hackneyed design solutions such as logos based on globes to show internationality or logos based on Leonardo da Vinci's 'man as a measure' to show humanity and tradition. Logos can, with use, become extremely valuable and enduring assets but, like names, they need to be carefully contrived, appropriately differentiated, properly protected and skilfully communicated.

Developing packaging

Packaging design is important in communicating messages to consumers as to a product's quality, value and origin. In some instances it will be necessary (or at least advisable) for the designer to follow an existing packaging convention. (In mixer drinks, for example, tonic water normally has a yellow label, soda water a black and white label and bitter lemon a turquoise/green label.) At other times the designer will have considerable freedom to create a totally fresh visual identity that will allow the product to stand out from all the others on the shelf.

As with all other aspects of brands, however, a key factor in packaging design is the maintenance of consistency, of a visual *gestalt*. Companies such as Heinz, Bird's Eye and Campbell's have developed over decades a visual recognition system which identifies their products unequivocally and provides reassurance to the consumer faced with bewildering choice. The packaging designer needs to be sensitive to such design conventions and may often need to resist the urge to create totally new visual experiences.

The key elements in packaging design are normally the product name presented in a distinctive typeface, other supporting design elements, plus the structural elements of the pack. The designer has to work these elements together into a cohesive whole. However, the single most important element in communicating with the consumer is the use of the brand name, and any pack design should clearly honour the name by giving it pride of place and helping it stand out from the surrounding visual elements. The brand name should have visual impact and not be overwhelmed by other elements of the pack design or by competitive pack designs.

Besides the brand name, the package designer has to consider additional important elements including the product description, the product illustration, contents information, the bar code and so on. These various themes need to be integrated in such a way as to produce a distinctive and aesthetically satisfying whole. Finally, the physical packaging has a specific job to do in protecting the product during shipping, keeping it in optimum condition and preventing tampering, abuse and damage. Generally, packaging is a price-sensitive area; packages are produced in enormous volumes and differences of a fraction of a penny in the packaging cost may have a substantial impact on the profitability of the brand owner. The selection and design of the physical packaging is therefore of critical importance and needs to be undertaken with close regard to budgets and profit objectives. The cost implications of the choice of physical packaging, however, go way beyond simply the cost of buying the packaging. Other costs such as those of filling, closure systems, shipping and damage need also to be considered and these can, when added together, be far more important than the initial cost of the package itself. Glass containers, for example, might be relatively inexpensive to buy but if they lead to considerable extra breakage and spillage they may well prove to be a false economy.

Redesigning packaging

It is important when redesigning packaging not to destroy valuable visual equities which may exist in a brand – a distinctively shaped 'shield' (as with Heinz), a valuable colour (as with Coca-Cola or Kodak) or a package shape (as with Marmite).

It can be useful to analyse all the features of an existing package design into those which are inviolable and which should be changed only after the most careful consideration; those features which are important in supporting the key visual elements but which are tolerant of substantial change (e.g. product illustrations) and those which are relatively inconsequential in visual terms but which are required for statutory, marketing or distribution reasons (e.g. bar codes, recipes, ingredients, nutrition information).

The most important task is to identify clearly the 'inviolable' packaging features, agree these and ensure that they feature appropriately in the redesigned packaging so that the handover from the old packaging to the new is smooth and so that all the existing visual equity is retained. (Several packaging design consultancies have developed techniques which seek to identify and measure visual equities and categorise them as either inviolable, discretionary or technical.)

10
Developing corporate identities

The corporation is, in effect, a brand – it needs to present itself in a controlled, appropriate and differentiated fashion so as to assume in the minds of its various audiences a coherent and appropriate brand personality. Naturally, corporations seek to communicate with their audiences in a variety of ways and, like human personalities, they present themselves in somewhat different ways to different audiences even though the overall personality profile should be integrated, appropriate and appealing. The many ways in which a corporation addresses its audiences include briefings for journalists and industry analysts, corporate advertising, annual reports, civic and community activities and, of course, through the products and services that it offers. One critical factor, however, in all such communication is the visual identity that the corporation presents.

What is corporate identity?

The corporate identity is, in effect, the branding and packaging of an entire company, and the core of a good identity programme is to capture a company's style and personality and to communicate these to its various audiences. The personality of the company needs to be presented and positioned in a unique and memorable way; when done properly, corporate identity can become a powerful strategic weapon, one which can benefit a company in all aspects of its activities.

A company's corporate identity is a communications system which uses a repetition of visual elements to make a clear and unambiguous statement about the company. Companies interface with their various audiences in many different ways. A large company for example, may have hundreds of different vehicles of all types and sizes, all of which can be used to project positive statements about the company; the company will also have thousands of employees, many different factories or retail outlets, perhaps tens of thousands of shareholders, hosts of suppliers and, of course, an enormous customer base.

British Airways provides an example of the very many ways in which a single company can interact and communicate with its audiences. British Airways was privatised in 1987 and now has both institutional and private investors. It relates to these investors through annual reports, proxy forms, earnings statements and notices to shareholders. British Airways is also a major purchaser of products and services: it is a massive consumer of jet fuel, of all types of food and drink and of a host of other consumable, engineering and related products and services. The airline also interfaces on a wide scale with the general public – it advertises to them, competes for their business and flies them around the world. An individual working for a company like Shell or Pratt and Whitney or Saatchi and Saatchi would be quite likely to meet British Airways in a number of different guises: as a supplier to the company, as a private customer, as a shareholder, or as part of the audience for British Airways' advertisements and promotional material. That one person will deal with British Airways at a number of different levels but should have no confusion whatsoever that one single organisation is involved. Clearly, the nature of the relationship is different if one is negotiating the supply of replacement fan blades for jet engines from that if one is a Club World passenger flying to Hong Kong. Nevertheless, it is important for British Airways that it presents itself in a coherent and integrated fashion wherever it touches the life of that executive. There would, for example, be little point in British Airways trying to present a caring and friendly image in the business class cabin if the executive knew the company to be bullying and unpleasant in its buying activities (which does not, of course, mean that it cannot be professional and realistic in those activities). Similarly, investors in the company would not believe that the company was efficiently run, whatever the annual report said, if their own experience when flying with British Airways was of an utter shambles.

Corporations, therefore, need to project a consistent image which is appropriate and believable to all its various audiences, though, of course, the precise message will vary from audience to audience. Underpinning and reinforcing this message is a consistent and coherent corporate identity, a visual identity system which links together the many activities of the company and presents them to consumers in an integrated way.

The experience of Rover

It is not, of course, just the visual identity system which needs to be cohesive. Consumers need to understand how a company fits together; if they perceive a sense of order in a company then confidence and trust are enhanced. Both naming systems and visual identity systems contribute to the overall corporate identity and the best visual identity system will fail if the underlying structure is not comprehensible to consumers: they will view the visual identity system merely as window dressing.

Some years ago, before Rover adopted the Mini, Metro, Maestro, Montego naming system which it used throughout the 1980s, the company conducted research into the naming systems used by competitive car manufacturers. At that time Rover was only starting to pull together into a single, coherent whole the quite separate companies and divisions which had been merged to form the original British Leyland, later to become Austin Rover and then Rover. The research it conducted showed that the lack of cohesiveness in the group and the consequent lack of cohesiveness in the brand naming system were quite clearly recognised by consumers. The products of the company had names such as Dolomite, Marina, Mini, Stag and Allegro, and no overall naming or branding strategy existed. Ford, on the other hand, had a much more integrated and comprehensible approach – its cars had names like Cortina, Granada and Fiesta; though certain of their product names (e.g. Escort and Capri) did not quite fit into the system, nonetheless respondents in the research were quick to recognise that 'Ford has its act together', 'Ford knows what it is doing'. In contrast, the lack of branding cohesiveness within Rover was instantly recognised by consumers and confirmed for them their underlying fears about the company and its products.

In 1979 the company started to implement a systematic branding approach (the Mini, Metro, Maestro, Montego system as used for Austin

94

cars) and subsequently adopted a numeric system for Rover-branded vehicles. These branding initiatives helped in a significant way to adress the company's image problem. Once consumers started to perceive that the company had adopted a coherent naming strategy they started to believe that its activities in other areas – production, design, quality control, service, etc. – were receiving similar careful attention.

The visual identity of a company acts in exactly the same way. Consumers are not overly bothered as to whether a company has a coherent visual system: that is the company's business. If, however, no coherent system exists, this is subconsciously recognised by the consumer who interprets the lack of cohesiveness as representing a lack of order, structure and direction in the company. Conversely, companies who have strong and appropriate corporate identity systems are much more highly regarded because such systems imply cohesiveness, efficient management, good direction and an overall sense of order.

The need for consistency

To convey a sense of order through the corporate identity it is essential that the identity (and of course the company itself) in fact has a sense of order. Any corporate identity system must therefore be carefully worked out, and the system needs to specify exactly how it operates at all levels in the organisation. The implementation of the system also needs to be closely controlled and monitored. Any corporation-wide system will be used in so many places and in so many applications that the opportunities for distortion and corruption of the identity are enormous.

Inevitably, however, any corporate identity system will need to be reviewed from time to time. Companies operate in an environment of constant change and no corporate identity system can ever be so well designed that it never needs to be altered.

Overhauling the identity

Changes to corporate identity systems can take two forms. Firstly, it can be reviewed and updated periodically but the key underlying visual components of the system left unchanged. For example, during the course of the last one hundred years the visual identity of Shell has been overhauled perhaps ten or a dozen times but the famous logo has remained fundamentally unchanged. The present-day Coca-Cola logo, too, is essentially the same (despite updating and modernisation) as that first used in Atlanta, Georgia in 1886. (The original logo used a form of copperplate handwriting so that the two words were shown with distinctive, flowing Cs.)

Generally, when a corporate identity system is being reviewed it is desirable to preserve, as far as possible, the existing visual equity. After all, it is extremely expensive, time consuming and difficult to establish visual equity and it should not be discarded purely on a whim. At times, however, corporations go through periods of such change that it is clearly inappropriate to use either the former identity or name. This can happen, for example, after mergers when choosing to retain the name or corporate identity of one party to the detriment of the other might imply an imbalance that may be unfair or inappropriate. It can happen too that when a company changes the nature of its business it can find itself with a name and corporate identity which are now inappropriate. In such instances the company may have no choice but to develop a new name and identity from scratch. In practice, although such a task may appear daunting, a change of corporate name often provides companies with an unmatched opportunity to address itself to its audiences, explain the reasons for change and talk about its plans for the future. The precise way in which the 'baton change' is handled from the old identity to the new is, however, critical.

Developing a new identity

The task of developing a new corporate name and corporate identity parallels that of developing a new brand name and brand identity. In selecting the name care needs to be taken that the new name is appropriate both now and in the foreseeable future both in one's home market and internationally. It must also be suitable for all the uses to which it will be put, and acceptable to all the company's many audiences. Equally importantly, it must be available for use and protectable both as a corporate name and, normally, as a trade mark in those product or service classes where the company is active or likely to be active.

It is sometimes tempting, particularly in those companies where the corporate name is used only on a limited scale and where the branding systems employed are dominated by product or divisional names, to think that the corporate name and identity are of little significance. In fact, even in companies where the corporate name and identity do not reach down to the consumer it is still seen by, and imparts messages to, a variety of audiences and is important even in such relatively specialised situations.

In all companies, then, a properly constructed, thorough, well implemented corporate identity system helps position the company and its products, assists in communication and motivation, imparts messages to both suppliers and investors, focuses the power of the media, ensures the proper participation of subsidiaries, divisions and operating companies, and ensures that the overall aims and direction of the company are well understood.

11
Managing brands

The concept of brand management as a separate staff function within an organisation is fairly new, emerging only after the Second World War. The history of brand management in a major (hypothetical) branded goods company might typically be as described below.

Brand management in a major foods group: the history of Omega Foods

The Omega Foods Company is a major food group which can trace its origins to the early part of the nineteenth century, although until the 1920s and 1930s the various constituent parts of the company were all separate, family-controlled businesses. For a number of reasons – lack of natural succession in the family, the effect of the 1929 crash, increasing competition, etc. – a number of the major constituent parts of the present group started to merge at this time and the current group structure can quite clearly be traced back to these early days.

Until the mid 1960s the new grouping had little impact on the brands. The various companies all operated more-or-less independently and each business had its own board of directors, its own factories, its own sales force and its own brands. True, the general manager of each operating company sat on the board of the group company but the group board was mainly concerned with new acquisitions, setting up factories abroad and with profits and dividends. All the real action was in the operating companies.

Brand management in Omega Foods

There was at this time no system of brand management as such. It simply was not needed. For example, the general manager of a canning company in the group, Stannards of Beccles, was in fact a member of the Stannard family. Stannard's had only one brand – Stannard's itself – and everyone involved in the business lived, breathed and (literally) ate the Stannard's brand. Every member of the company was in a sense a Stannard's brand manager, not least the general manager himself.

In the mid-1960s things started to change. A giant American foods company started to show an interest in acquiring Omega Foods. Although the American predator was seen off fairly quickly, the half-hearted takeover attempt sent a shiver of apprehension through the Omega Foods board.

Other changes were also underway. Grocers like Jack Cohen and the Sainsbury family were starting to form powerful retail groups and Omega Foods had already appointed at the centre a national sales manager to handle all such large accounts, thus eroding the autonomy of the operating companies. The company had also set up a central research and development laboratory, and the overseas companies, which were now thriving, produced for their domestic markets the products of all the UK operating companies. They demonstrated quite clearly that 'dedicated' marketing teams and sales forces were not necessary for success – one sales force, for example, could quite comfortably handle all the group's products.

In 1967 a major reorganisation took place. The old head office in the City was closed and group headquarters moved to a new, purpose-built office block thirty miles outside London. At the same time all the sales forces were merged into one and now reported to a new group sales and marketing director. Also, a new central finance function was set up and a group production director was appointed who became responsible for all manufacturing worldwide.

The sales and marketing director appointed in 1967 had come to prominence because he had recognised early on that retailing in Britain was changing quickly. He had achieved remarkable success with the new, emerging multiples and represented a novel type of aggressive, driving executive quite different from the more traditional, production-orientated managers who compromised most of the company's management. Over the course of a few years he streamlined the sales force achieving substantial savings. However, even after the rationalisation of the sales forces into one national force the group still employed a direct sales team of almost three hundred people including area managers, regional managers, trainees and sales managers specialising in certain sectors (e.g. the armed services, the health service, airlines, institutional caterers, etc.) Inevitably, much of the focus of the sales and marketing function came to be directed towards managing and motivating this large and expensive resource and towards satisfying the needs of a few major customers who compromised a substantial (but minority) proportion of total sales.

All activities not concerned with direct selling or managing the sales force were delegated to a group marketing manager who was particularly involved with group advertising although he also handled public relations, the annual report, group literature, special promotions, training, some new product development and the brand managers.

The brand managers are based at head office and have virtually no contact with the manufacturing plants (the previously autonomous operating companies quickly became simply production units). In the early days after the reorganisation the brand managers were selected on the basis of their close knowledge of the brands. Over the years, however, a system grew up whereby brand management became a training ground for young high flyers, especially those joining the company as graduate trainees.

Brand management at Omega Foods is considered a glamorous and desirable job. Even the minor brands have quite large advertising budgets and the brand managers are viewed as important clients by the advertising agencies and by the various marketing services companies such as market research firms and sales promotion agencies. Generally, brand management at Omega Foods is felt to work reasonably well. The brands are relatively stable and do not have precipitous ups and downs. Within the advertising agency world Omega Foods is felt to be a fair dealer which employs competent brand managers and does a good, honourable job of looking after its brands.

Brand management problems

What does this typical case history tell us about brand management? Firstly, it is clear that the current system of brand management treats a brand largely as an abstraction, a concept. Brand managers are divorced from brand production and also, mainly, from selling. Their primary orientation is towards the maintenance of an intangible: the brand. Their success in doing so is normally measured in terms of market share.

This feature of current brand management can be regarded as being largely positive. Although the factory or operating company orientated approach might appear to result in an intense focus on the brand, this focus is, in reality, normally aimed mainly at the product itself and its manufacture and sale rather than at the brand. Under such a system the aim of advertising, for example, is to shift products, not to build brands, and the overall purpose of branding is frequently viewed as being to distinguish one supplier's products from those of others through labelling. Although there might be intense pride in the product and the label, such an approach often fails to appreciate, except subconsciously, that the brand has a distinct personality and presents unique opportunities for the development of consumer loyalties and for line extension.

Further benefits of the current brand management system lie in such areas as buying (where a concentration of buying power can lead to economies in such areas as advertising, marketing research, print, etc.) and the development of a consistent brand culture.

However, current brand management procedures often present profound problems too. Firstly, the individual brand manager is usually at a junior level, may have relatively limited business experience and frequently therefore does not yet possess the authority, experience or maturity to perform effectively a complex role involving elements of analysis, creativity, co-ordination, persuasion and leadership. The brand manager role is, arguably, one of the most difficult in the company. The brand manager has responsibilities, but little authority, and is concerned with large turnovers, substantial profits and substantial expenditures. The brand manager also has to liaise internally with production, R&D, finance and sales. It is clearly a role which is highly responsible and which demands maturity and interpersonal skills of a high order. Junior executives, perhaps only a year or two out of college and with only limited business experience (and that in a direct sales function), understandably often find brand management a difficult and frustrating role to perform.

Moreover, the organisation itself frequently does little to help. Brand management is normally an amorphous staff role with ill-defined reporting relationships, objectives, responsibilities or targets. All too often, brand managers are merely perceived as link people, the interface with the advertising agency. They are not seen as having any true management role whatsoever but merely as fulfilling a co-ordinating function. A familiar pattern emerges. Brand management is regarded as a staging post for young high flyers. They are selected for their potential and apparent 'flair', often being identified as 'agency types', people who are comfortable in the 'glamorous' world of advertising. To such people the mundane world of head office, of budgets, capital appropriations and marginal costings can quickly become tedious, especially when agency lunches, approval visits to locations for television commercials and meetings with national personalities to discuss advertising scripts have become the norm. All too often the young brand manager slips into the role of simply serving as a link with the advertising agency (something that most people in the company see, in any case, as the main purpose of the job), enjoying more being courted by the agency than dealing with the rather more tedious aspects of brand management. In effect, one component of the brand management job comes to dominate all others. Young brand managers are, however, usually idealistic and far from corrupt and have a keen interest in representing the interests of their companies and in being seen to do so. All newly appointed brand managers quickly realise that they can demonstrate their independence by inviting several agencies to pitch for the account and appointing an entirely new agency.

Naturally, no new agency pitching for an account will give unequivocal approval to what has gone before. If the previous advertising veered towards the traditional it will be accused of being staid and a 'contemporary' approach will be advocated. If the advertising has been following a more contemporary theme there will be a call for a return to traditional values. The result is that the positioning of the brand may well adopt an erratic path – every few years the agency is changed along with the packaging and the advertising message. Occasionally the brand manager can claim a major success; more usually the company is left with a brand which is damaged by periodic tinkering while the brand manager moves onwards and upwards, often to a new job outside the company.

The tendency for brand managers to function merely in a liaison role is exacerbated by the fact that few companies employ any kind of brand accounting. The financial information made available to brand managers normally consists of little more than raw sales data (tonnages, sales by region, etc.) together with data on advertising expenditure, gross margins, etc. The marketing department will normally supplement this with market research and tracking data but often the overall picture is so unreliable and discredited that the brand manager (who, after all, has been selected largely on the basis of his or her ability to see the larger picture and not get too bogged down in detail) has little difficulty in discrediting all 'hard' data and instead makes all brand decisions largely on the basis of hunch, flair, anecdote and intuition.

The myth of the modern brand management system is of a cadre of hardened branding professionals fanatically devoted to their brands, who understand them intimately and who single-mindedly champion 'their' brands at all levels in the organisation. The actuality is usually, though not always, somewhat different – a group of rather inexperienced but well-intentioned people who are provided with little information or guidance, who are relatively junior in the company, who have ill-defined reporting relationships and responsibilities, and who struggle to do their best against the odds, often settling for a role which is primarily concerned with agency liaison.

Principles of brand management

From the earliest times farmers have been aware that certain rules of husbandry need to be followed in order to produce good, consistent yields. However, those rules were by no means widely understood or adhered to, and it was not until the eighteenth century that the basic rules of husbandry were drawn together into a set of principles which transcended individual prejudices and preferences. Once the need for crop rotation, seed selection and good fertilising methods was widely understood, productivity increased enormously and the risks of crop failure were much reduced.

A similar situation exists today in respect of brands and brand husbandry. The general nature of brands is well understood and certain companies – Procter and Gamble, Unilever and Mars are examples – have developed particularly good brand management techniques. However, such techniques are by no means widely used by brand-owning companies and policies are frequently adopted in all good faith

103

which are detrimental to both the short- and longer-term health of the brand. What, then, are the basic rules of good brand husbandry?

Brand-centricity

Once we accept that, for very many companies, their most valuable and important assets are their brands, it becomes clear that they should develop a style and structure which recognises this fact and which focuses the company on the proper management, development and exploitation of these assets. This focus is referred to as brand-centricity.

The first organisational function which requires attention is, obviously, the brand management function. Brand management is a vital function in most organisations but the status and authority of brand management within the organisation and the quality of information flowing to brand managers often needs much improvement. In many branded goods companies there is a strong case for turning the marketing director into the brands director.

The accounting function, too, needs to be organised to produce financial information on a brand-by-brand basis and not merely on a geographical, divisional or production unit basis. Similarly, investment in brand building needs to be treated just as carefully and analytically as any other major corporate investment decision. The switching of resources out of or between brands needs to be subject to in-depth analysis and the differential performance and sensitivity of brands should be accurately monitored.

Other parts of the organisation also need to be made more brand-centric. While it might be appropriate to retain a conventional organisation structure (for example, marketing, sales, manufacturing, R&D, financial, personnel) the importance and value of brands needs to be made manifest throughout the organisation. In R&D, for example, a clearer understanding of each brand's positioning, appeals, strengths, weaknesses and threats may well lead to a more focused R&D programme. One of the key tasks of a brands director would be to ensure that brands receive an appropriate share of attention in all functional areas.

Of course, to advocate the adoption of a brand-centric approach is not to deny the importance of the sales force or the production and R&D departments. Rather, if a company's most valuable assets are its brands and if its most potent weapons for securing and maintaining market share, achieving distribution, gaining sales and earning margin and profits are its brands, then the brands must permeate that organisation. The accounts department must account for brands, R&D must help to develop new and improved branded products, and so forth. Brand-centricity, therefore, merely recognises the actuality of the situation for many companies.

Conservative management

It is extremely expensive to establish a new consumer brand. Even in a single geographical market like the United Kingdom, a new brand generally needs a launch budget of millions of pounds before major retailers can be persuaded to stock it. The cost of launching international brands is very much higher. It also takes a long time, several years at minimum, before the brand achieves any certainty of longer-term survival. It may take even longer before the brand gets into the black. Finally, launching new brands is exceptionally risky – the vast majority of new brands fail. Once a brand is established, however, it is normally a robust asset and one with the likelihood, if properly cared for, of a long life.

The reason why it is such a costly and drawn-out process to establish a brand, particularly in consumer markets where the physical character-istics of products are increasingly similar, is that there is much competition for the consumer's loyalty and attention. Moreover, the brand owner is seeking to establish a bond between the consumer and the brand when, initially at least, the consumer may have little interest in the brand and has more than enough other things with which to be concerned. Once 'bonding' takes place, however, its hold can be very strong. However, as in any relationship each side must keep its part of the bargain. It is often the case that it is the consumer (initially the more reluctant of the two parties) who is more constant in his or her loyalties to the brand than the brand owner. The brand owner is likely to tinker with the brand, change the message, change the packaging, change the formulation, often it seems without good reason and without reference to the preferences of the consumer.

The conservative management of brands, is therefore advisable. Brand owners must recognise that brands are rare and precious assets

105

and that they deserve to be treated with care and consideration. The danger signals indicating that brand management is out of control, and that the essential values and qualities of the brand are not clearly understood and communicated include frequent changes of advertising agency and communications message, radical packaging changes where the old 'visual equity' is discarded, inappropriate brand extension, stop–start promotional budgets and strong swings from above-the-line to below-the-line promotions.

This is not to suggest that all brand repositioning exercises, all changes of agency, all line extensions and all package redesigns are causes for concern because clearly they are not: brands, like anything else, must adapt or die. Rather, change for change's sake or because the brand manager is bored or is focused on personal career requirements and not the good of the brand are all inappropriate. If the change is unsuccessful it is the brand owner who will have to pay the price in the end.

Define the brand

An essential prerequisite of successful brand management is to have a precise, agreed definition of the brand, its critical points of difference from competitive brands and the satisfactions the brand delivers. A brand 'blueprint' should be prepared and agreed for each of the company's brands. It should be essentially qualitative and detail the personality and positioning of the brand, as well as containing standards for all physical packaging, signage and so forth in much the same way that a corporate identity manual does for the visual expression of a corporate personality. This brand blueprint should then be circulated to all those involved in the management of the brand including the brand manager, the R&D department, the advertising agency and the package designers. Naturally, this blueprint will be subject to challenge and will need constant updating. It will nonetheless serve as a fixed point for all brand-related decisions.

All too often, in the absence of an agreed brand blueprint and clearly defined brand strategy we find that those involved in the management of the brand have attitudes and plans for a brand which are by no means in step. The brand manager wishes the brand to be positioned as fresh, contemporary and of the moment, and briefs the advertising agency to achieve this positioning; the sales force, on the other hand, perceive the brand as a 'staple', a product which any retailer must stock and which affords the brand owner the opportunity to sell to the retailer other brands; the finance department see the brand as a 'cash cow' and is loathe to spend money on brand development. These discontinuities between the perceptions of various groups involved in the management and exploitation of the brand become much more serious when brand management changes fairly frequently and each new brand manager has to define for him or herself precisely what is this brand they are now responsible for. Under the circumstances it is not surprising that brand management practices are often highly erratic and damaging to the brand.

And what of the consumer? Consumers often object strongly to having 'their' brands 'tinkered with' – witness the Coca-Cola/Coke/Classic Coke furore in the United States when Coca-Cola tried to reformulate the product to meet the increasing threat from Pepsi-Cola. This is not to say that brand development is undesirable. It is, in fact, essential, but must be handled conservatively and sensitively. By agreeing a brand blueprint, installing programmes for its review and ensuring that unauthorised departures from the blueprint are not permitted, the opportunities for erratic brand management policies and subsequent brand abuse will be much reduced. Managers who wish to alter any element of the brand will need to justify their action on grounds other than mere hunch or whim.

Structures of branding

Various types of branding structure are used by companies and no universally ideal model exists: each company must develop a branding structure to suit its particular needs.

There is, however, increased interest by companies in an 'endorsed' approach to branding whereby new brands are endorsed by an existing corporate brand whose equity acts as a lever to the new brand. The difficulty with such 'hybrid' branding systems is that they require particularly close control and great sureness of touch. There is a considerable danger that the house brand will be used arbitrarily on any number of new products without proper consideration and control, that brand managers will use it as a kind of buoyancy aid, refusing to relinquish it even when its positive contribution is long gone, and that the net result will be the failure to achieve a truly free-standing product brand and a dilution of the valuable equity in the house brand.

Ten rules of good brand management

Ten simple rules of good brand management can be established from the above discussion.

1. *Cherish your brands.* Ensure that your brands are cared for. Treat them as valuable and important assets. Ensure that they have a central role in the organisation.
2. *Take brand management seriously.* Treat it as a senior function and give it authority and responsibility.
3. *Account for your brands.* Adopt brand accounting otherwise you will have no idea as to the financial performance of your brands and will not be able to make informed, brand-related decisions.
4. *Manage your brands conservatively.* Have a clear idea as to each brand's personality and positioning. Do not tinker with your brands unless there is a good reason for doing so.
5. *Maintain responsibility for your brands.* It is foolish to surrender responsibility for your brands to an advertising agency. Although agencies are honourable and dedicated they are not skilled in brand management and by no means always share precisely the same objectives as their clients.
6. *Maintain a point of difference in each brand.* Remember that customers have many brands to choose from; give them a reason to choose yours.
7. *Exploit the equity in your brands.* Brand extension is a legitimate and sensible activity but care needs to be exercised to avoid brand dilution (see Chapter 12).
8. *Review your portfolio.* Brands are increasingly being viewed as separable, transferable assets (see Chapter 16). You should consider disposing of brands that do not fit your portfolio and replacing them with others that do.
9. *Consider the international implications for your brand.* The internationalisation of branding makes it important to think beyond national boundaries, otherwise your brand runs the risk of being overrun by a more aggressive foreign competitor.

Ten rules of good brand management

10. *Protect your brands*. Trade mark registration affords powerful rights at low cost (See Chapter 14). You should ensure that you have clear title to your brands in all countries and in all categories of goods likely to be of interest.

Perhaps surprisingly, these rather obvious rules are broken time and again – brand responsibility is devolved to agencies, international opportunities and threats are ignored until it is too late, trade mark problems are swept under the carpet. However, there are signs of change. Brand valuation, for example, confers an entirely new status on the brand which, in the longer term, is bound to transform the practice of brand management.

12
Brand extension

Developing new brands is extremely expensive, highly risky and takes a long time. The *expense* of new brand development results not just from the cost of identifying and validating a new brand concept, from developing and protecting the new brand name, and from creating the packaging, but also from the fact that heavy advertising is needed to launch a brand and to support it over the first months and years of its life. In such areas as toiletries, food and drink it is now virtually impossible to launch a new brand without a multi-million pound advertising campaign. Moreover, a short-term launch campaign is far from sufficient to establish a new brand. The process of branding is one whereby a bond is created between the brand and the consumer and, generally the consumer has little interest, at least initially, in the brand proposition. Sustained advertising and promotional investment is therefore required to create this bond and reassure the consumer that the brand proposition will endure; such on-going support is expensive.

Riskiness, the second problem of new brand development, is evident from the fact that the majority of new brands are seen to fail. However, unreliable data and lack of diagnostic information make the real reasons for failure difficult to determine. The fault may lie in one or several areas of inadequacy, including the brand concept, brand support, distribution systems, the company's available resources or its resolve.

The third problem for new brand development is the *time* that it takes to develop a new brand. Sustained investment is needed to establish a brand in the consumer's mind and it is likely that many of the brand failures already referred to can be attributed to the fact that the brand owner did not have the resources or nerve to support his brand over an extended period of time. Generally, new brand development should be viewed in terms of three to five years.

All these factors combine to create a strong and growing interest in brand extension. The arguments in favour of brand extension, as opposed to new brand development, are that it reduces risk, reduces cost and reduces the time involved in getting a new product onto the market. Brand extension can also maintain interest in an existing brand and may help to ensure that it remains relevant and contemporary in a changing world. The arguments against brand extension are that in certain instances it can actually dilute the equity which exists in a brand and thus seriously hazard the brand. What then are the considerations in brand extension?

Reasons for brand extension

In the early 1980s, Beecham found itself under considerable short-term profit pressure. Financial journalists began to tip Beecham as an acquisition target and considerable speculation arose as to the long-term survival of the company as an independent business. Faced with this problem, considerable changes took place in the management of the group. One major initiative was in the area of brands. Beecham had long been known as a company with a portfolio of valuable brands and with particular skills in brand management. As a result of the external pressures placed on it, Beecham was forced to reappraise the husbandry of its brands and decided that certain were underutilised assets which were capable of considerable extension. The brands involved included Ribena, Lucozade and Brylcreem, and in the space of only three or four years the market position, perceptions and the fortunes of these brands were transformed. Ribena, for example, had traditionally been positioned as a nourishing blackcurrant drink for young children. New flavours and pack sizes were introduced and the brand was repositioned as a range of refreshing, healthy, natural fruit drinks for people of all ages.

Lucozade received a similar treatment. For decades Lucozade had been sold as a glucose drink to aid the recovery of sick children. The drink was dramatically, but entirely plausibly, repositioned as a healthy sports drink for people of all ages. Daley Thompson, the Olympic decathlon champion, was used to endorse the brand and the images of the sick room were entirely left behind. New flavour formulas, packaging formats and pack sizes were introduced and sales increased massively. In the space of only two to three years the brand was successfully established in completely new market sectors, and at modest cost.

Brylcreem, a hair gel, is a brand which has strong associations with male grooming although, until recently, it has been perceived as largely rooted in the inter-war and immediate post-war period. Only a few years ago it would have seemed unlikely that the brand could be successfully revived and extended. In fact, although Brylcreem's success has not yet matched that of Ribena and Lucozade, by redesigning the packaging, introducing a new range of male grooming and toiletry products under the Brylcreem name and by repositioning the brand in an altogether more contemporary and appealing fashion, the apparently terminal decline in the brand's fortunes has been halted. Indeed, it seems possible that the brand may yet be re-established as a mainstream product in its sector, this time with a much wider brand franchise. Beecham has therefore extended and repositioned the Brylcreem brand to secure profitable sales at low cost and low risk; it has also been able to move much more quickly by using a brand extension strategy.

Factors in brand extension

The key factor in brand extension is to have a clear picture of the core values embodied by the brand and a clear plan for exploiting the brand's equity in a consistent and methodical fashion. Beecham recognised that Lucozade was not a pharmaceutical product but rather was a healthy and nutritious drink. It focused on these key attributes and successfully extended the brand by introducing a positioning which consumers found entirely credible.

Similarly, the elegance, sophistication, style and precision engineering characteristics of a Porsche car can be entirely plausibly transposed to Porsche watches, Porsche sunglasses, even perhaps to Porsche clothing, cameras or luggage. Any brand extensions of the Porsche name which maintain the essential attributes of style, sophistication and high quality are appropriate and credible, and all would serve to develop the brand and not to damage it.

Where extension has proved damaging to brands is where the essential qualities and attributes of the brand have been only imperfectly understood. In the 1950s Rolls-Royce supplied motor car engines to Austin for installation in a relatively inexpensive limousine called the Austin Princess. Austin were allowed to use the Rolls-Royce name in promoting their new cheap limousine but the collaboration proved a massive failure as it debased the Rolls-Royce brand and the juxtaposition of Rolls-Royce and Austin was not credible.

In the 1970s Imperial Foods, the then owners of the HP brand, undertook a brand extension initiative which was similarly ill-judged. Considering that the essential feature of the HP brand name was the fact that it connoted high quality sauces to complement foods of all types, the company introduced a range of ice-cream toppings under the HP name. This attempt at brand extension proved disastrous. In fact, the HP brand was overwhelmingly associated only with savoury sauces, and the extension of the brand to sweet sauces was considered by consumers to be entirely inappropriate. Indeed, it transpired that to many consumers the idea of putting HP sauce on ice-cream was felt to be almost repulsive.

Thus the key factor in line extension is to understand clearly the particular values, attributes and personality of the brand. Only then can thought be given to those areas in which these attributes could be applied. Furthermore, it should be borne in mind that the process of line extension can, if necessary, be undertaken gradually; such an approach allows extension into product sectors that would be impossible to penetrate if the extension were to be attempted in a single leap.

The Dunhill brand provides an excellent example of gradual extension. Dunhill is not only a leading cigarette brand but also one of the leading world brands in the area of luxury products and accessories for men and, more recently, women. Dunhill started as a cigarette brand which was then extended to embrace smoking accessories (pipes, pouches, lighters, etc.). Once the brand was established in areas immediately adjacent to the core, it was extended again into other male accessories (belts, desktop items, cufflinks, clothing, etc.) and most recently the brand has been extended again into male fragrances and mainstream fashion items. Moreover, all this has been achieved without in any way damaging the equity of the original brand; in fact, the reverse is the case.

All brand owners should consider their brands as potentially suitable for line extension and, indeed, if brands are not exploited in this way valuable assets are, potentially, being underutilised. Certainly, to embark on a process of new brand development with its accompanying costs and risks may be foolhardy if the same objective could be achieved through line extension.

Maintaining visual equities

A further factor in line extension, besides the maintenance of the core personality of the brand, is the maintenance of the brand's visual identity as the more generalised the brand becomes, and the more it is extended into new areas, the more it is necessary to maintain the overall integrity of the brand at all levels. Brand management under such circumstances becomes a particularly important and difficult task and the visual manifestation of the brand, including logos and packaging, needs to be carefully controlled. Companies such as Heinz and Campbell's have developed and adopted visual systems which allow for all new products sold under the house brand to be clearly identified without fear of confusion as to what each product is, yet at the same time the overall integrity and coherence of the brand is maintained. Conversely, in the absence of such a system, brand extension can result in a fragmentation of brand identity and personality which can seriously adversely affect the value and power of the core brand.

Maintaining brand boundaries

It is also important for brand owners to determine the boundaries of their brands so as to keep a check on uncontrolled brand extension. Precisely where these boundaries are located can, of course, be challenged, and if necessary they can be extended and modified. Thus when new product opportunities present themselves which fall outside the established boundaries for existing brands, the brand owner can consider whether to redefine the territory of an existing brand, develop a new brand or acquire an existing brand from another company – a practice which is becoming increasingly common.

13
International branding

When Gulliver was shipwrecked on Lilliput he found the population divided into two deeply antagonistic groups. There were those who broke their eggs at the round end and those who fervently supported the notion of only breaking eggs at the pointed end. Swift's tale was intended as a savage satire on eighteenth century British politics, but his satire could perhaps also be applied to the current 'global branding' debate.

Global versus local branding

Two quite separate views are often advocated by branding experts on the subject of international brands. The first, that of the proponents of global branding, has been most eloquently and forcefully stated by Saatchi and Saatchi and other major international agencies. Basically, their view is that international media overlaps, new technologies such as satellite broadcasting and a general coming together of consumer tastes will inevitably lead to the increased preponderance and power of global brands and that this will seriously disadvantage those brands which operate only on a national or local basis.

The opposite view, often expressed by nationally-based advertising agencies, is that the process of global branding leads to the development of homogenised *esperanto* brands which are so generalised that they lose their intimate appeal and positioning. In contrast, locally-based brands can be more closely adapted to meet the particular needs and requirements of local consumers. Thus local brands will always be more appealing, more responsive and potentially more successful than global brands.

It is easy to see how protagonists on each side of the debate have embraced the views which they have. Agencies such as Saatchi and Saatchi have a powerful international network and are capable of servicing most effectively those clients who favour the notion of global branding. The smaller local agencies in contrast are seriously disadvantaged when competing for such business and need instead to make a virtue out of their small size and local orientation.

What, then, is the future of branding? Are global brands akin to vast unmanoeuvrable supertankers which present certain efficiencies of scale but which are difficult to handle and unresponsive to the helm? Do local brands afford the possibility of closer adaptation to the particular needs of local populations?

The growth of international branding

International branding has grown steadily since the advent of modern branding one hundred or so years ago. American companies such as Ford, Kellogg's and General Foods, for example, have been producing and selling their branded products internationally for generations. British companies, too, have established their brands around the world. Dunlop, for example, (now mainly Japanese owned) has manufactured Dunlop brand tyres in such countries as Japan, the United States, France, Germany and Australia since the end of the last century. There can be no doubt, therefore, of the ability of brands to travel and of their potential power and appeal on an international basis. The reasons for this are many but come down to the fact that we all have a broad commonality of needs, wishes and interests irrespective of our nationality and local cultural differences. A bottle of Perrier provides the same refreshment to a Japanese consumer as it does to a French consumer; a Dunlop tyre does precisely the same job on a vehicle in Brazil as it does in Britain. There is a reasonable chance therefore that if a product is successfully developed and branded so as to appeal in one market it may well appeal in others. Of course, this is not universally true, and there are many examples of products that yet remain undesired or unappealing outside their home markets.

Advantages of international brands

The advantages of international brands to their owners are many. Firstly, such brands allow their owners to extend their brands from market to market relatively straightforwardly and inexpensively. The owner of a brand which has a brand name and general look which has been developed for international use can simply ship the brand into a new market, test its appeal there and, subsequently, develop that local market without massive investment in new brand development. The internationalisation of brands by building up from small-scale to large-scale importation and then to local production and supply has often developed from what was initially an export strategy. Indeed, this route has most recently been followed by many major Japanese companies who are now manufacturing their branded products abroad, whereas just a decade ago most of their production originated in Japan.

The owner of an international brand can also benefit in overseas markets from experience acquired so expensively in the home market. The brand owner does not, therefore, have to reinvent a new brand to suit local conditions and develop for the brand an entirely new positioning and set of attributes. Coca-Cola, for example, has developed in America a model of exactly how the Coca-Cola brand operates. This model embraces the product itself, its key differentiating features, the unique bottling and distribution system, the advertising and so forth. Although this model needs to be adjusted from one country to another to suit local conditions and preferences, nonetheless the basic structure and values remain and permit ready international development.

Owners of international brands are able, therefore, to reap benefits of scale as the experience they gain in one market can be exploited in others. In addition, real benefits accrue in areas such as production. In Europe, for example, if manufacturers focus exclusively on a single national market they are confining themselves to relatively limited production runs. The whole concept behind the European Economic Community is to create a single market of 350 million wealthy consumers where previously a series of much smaller markets existed. The benefits of creating this single market are considered so obvious that the fundamental concept of the Single Market has hardly been challenged (at least not in so far as the potential economic benefits are concerned) yet in order to take full advantage of such opportunities it is essential that manufacturers trade using international brands.

The tyre industry again provides a good example of the way in which international brands permit the more ready exploitation of international markets. A tyre manufacturer producing a new range of branded products may well decide, in response to an order from Fiat, to site all its production of twelve inch tyres at its Italian tyre plant. Later, when orders come in from Volvo and British Leyland for the same size of tyre, these too will be sourced from Italy. Similarly, fourteen inch tyres may well be built in Germany, ten inch tyres in Britain and so on. The economies of production are substantial but require at the same time an internationalisation of branding – there would be no point in having a proliferation of different brand names as the economies involved in the production process would be largely wasted.

A further powerful influence in favour of international branding is the internationalisation of media and communications. Formula One motor races are now broadcast live into millions of homes around the world wherever they take place. Brand owners such as Benetton, Marlboro, American Express, Honda, Goodyear and ICI use Formula One motorsport to promote their brands knowing that their sponsorship will reach world audiences. It is obviously sensible to ensure that the brands concerned are truly international or else the promotion is partly wasted, as is currently true of the promotion of Cabin cigarettes, a brand owned by Japan Tobacco. Being virtually unknown outside Japan, the benefits to the company of its motor racing sponsorship are much diminished. The growth of satellite television is certain to increase media overlaps sharply and, hence, encourage the current trend towards international branding.

Another factor leading to the internationalisation of brands is the worldwide phenomenon of increased travel. In the British case, the first cheap package tours (to the Spanish Mediterranean coast) only started in the 1960s. Now, a substantial minority of British people travel abroad at least once a year and find reassurance in international brands such as Heineken and Hertz. Thus the brand loyalties they have developed in one market can be transferred to another.

International branding is, therefore, an established phenomenon and one which trends in international communications, media overlaps, travel and the growth of language skills (particularly the use of English) seem certain to encourage. Political factors too will continue to play a powerful part in increasing the internationalisation of brands. The European Economic Community is not the only trading group which is being established in the world at present. Efforts are being made, with varying success, to establish similar trading groups in South America, the Caribbean and elsewhere and the tariff barriers which currently serve to protect local brands are being increasingly torn down such that the free flow of goods between markets is now a new reality.

Other factors

There are, however, two further factors which are leading manufacturers to develop international as opposed to local brands.

The first is the increasing segmentation of markets. Companies such as Henkel of West Germany, a major manufacturer of detergents and do-it-yourself products, has argued powerfully that as market sectors become narrower and as consumers become more discerning in their choice of products, it becomes increasingly difficult for manufacturers to justify the development of new brands which only serve a local market. Although one possible exception to this trend is provided by the United States (a market so huge and homogeneous that local manufacturers can develop brands purely for their home market and ignore other areas of the world), this strategy, Henkel argues, is not open to manufacturers of branded products outside the United States. The only way for such manufacturers to justify new brand development, the development of advertising and packaging and the establishment of production capacity is on the basis of international markets. Local markets simply cannot provide the volume to justify the development of closely targeted, specialised consumer brands.

The second, and often unrecognised, factor is that international brands afford their owners the means of maintaining a coherence to their affairs. When international branded goods businesses operate internationally under international brands they can manage their business around the world in a consistent and coherent fashion. If, on the other hand, they do not possess international brands, their business inevitably becomes highly fragmented even when they operate in the same product areas in different countries. The French subsidiary with its own local brands might, for example, develop its own range extensions, packaging and television commercials and would tend to operate largely autonomously; the British, German and Japanese companies would all do exactly the same. Head office may provide some sort of R&D service as well as other central services but essentially its role would be mainly that of a banker: approving capital expenditure, providing cash and collecting dividends. Any such group would have none of the coherence which is available to those companies which operate truly international brands.

Local brands

What, then, of the contention that international brands simply cannot have the close adaptation to local conditions and the flexibility and sure-footedness of local brands? This argument is unconvincing because it is based on a false premise: namely that international brands are not, or cannot be, adapted in local markets to suit local conditions. In practice, one of the key skills involved in international branding is to maintain an international coherence but, at the same time, to adapt the brand to suit local conditions. Coca-Cola containers, for example, are smaller in Japan than elsewhere as Japanese consumers are usually smaller than Americans and Europeans and do not wish to consume the same quantities of fluid. The cans, too, although they contain the identical product and have the same overall design as elsewhere, carry much of the detail in Chinese script and in katakana. The Coca-Cola Company does not, therefore, try to force on the Japanese consumer the identical product as is sold in Atlanta, Georgia.

Distribution arrangements for the Coca-Cola brand in Japan are also different in many respects from those which exist in the United States even though the basic franchised bottler system is common to both countries. For example, there cannot be many street blocks in Tokyo that do not have at least one vending machine for Coca-Cola soft drinks and many will have four or more machines. Coca-Cola has therefore quite clearly adapted the brand and its distribution to suit local conditions. Indeed, had Coca-Cola not recognised these local differences it would not be the success that it is in the Japanese market.

Examples of the local adaptation of international brands to suit particular local conditions abound. The Kellogg's Cornflakes pack in Britain is different in detail from that in the United States though the overall brand identity and brand proposition are quite clearly the same – there would, after all, be no point in Kellogg's making a special offer of a road atlas on its British cornflakes pack if the road atlas was one of North America.

The trend towards international brands

The trend towards the international branding of goods and services is likely to continue and indeed to strengthen. This, however, by no means precludes the need for sensitive brand positioning to suit local conditions.

Of course, not all brands have the potential to become international: many are limited by reason of local taste or preferences, though even here it is sensible to review the situation from time to time as brands which might currently be considered local and idiosyncratic might still provide opportunities for international development in the future. Other brands such as those in financial sectors might be prevented from becoming international due to local legislation or for other special reasons.

Developing international brands

What, then, is the process to be followed in order to develop international brands? Essentially, the disciplines and attitudes required are precisely the same as those needed for the development of national brands though with the addition of an international perspective. There is one particular matter, however, which in the case of international brands requires special attention: the brand name. It is essential, if a new brand has any prospect of international use, to establish a brand name at the outset which is suitable for use and protectable on an international basis: the brand name is not normally a matter which can be ignored and dealt with at a later date.

When developing a new brand it is not unusual for the entire focus of the exercise to be upon the immediate national market. This may be because the brand manager responsible has no international mandate or because the task of developing a brand to satisfy the international market is found to be so complex that to confuse the issue by adding an international perspective would be inappropriate. While it is easy to understand how this situation arises, it is nonetheless short-sighted to develop a new brand and launch it successfully in the home market only to find when the product is about to be launched internationally that the brand name is unsuitable for use or, most likely, legally unavailable abroad. The option of changing the brand name and identity in the original market no longer exists by then so the only option is to rebrand the product for international use. Once this decision is taken it is likely that the packaging will be changed dramatically as will the positioning, the advertising and so forth. All prospects of developing an international brand will have been destroyed because the brand name issue was not sorted out properly at the start. (Some companies have been able successfully to adopt an intermediate position. Unilever, for example, markets Oil of Ulay in Britain, and the brand carries different but similar names in other countries, for example Oil of Olaz. Despite having different but related brand names in different countries the product is still quite clearly an integrated international brand proposition.)

Even if the overwhelming focus of new brand development is on the home market, then, sensible minimum precautions should be taken to ensure that the brand name is checked as to suitability and availability in key overseas markets. If the brand is a failure in its home market the overseas trade mark applications can be allowed to lapse and little will have been lost. If, on the other hand, the brand proves a success, the brand owner can be confident of entering international markets under the same brand name and with the same overall brand proposition and overall look.

14
The legal side of brands

The assets of any business fall into two main categories: tangible and intangible. Tangible assets include plant, machinery, cash and property; intangible assets include intellectual property, relationships with suppliers and customers, the management team, the skilled workforce, clients lists, proprietary databases and so forth.

Intellectual property

The term 'intellectual property' is used to cover particular forms of intangible asset, principally trade marks, patents, copyrights and registered designs. These intangible assets, the product of the intellect, are important and valuable forms of property and, in legal terms, can be every bit as strong as tangible property. Thus they can be bought, sold, loaned and licensed and, in many respects, they are directly comparable with other forms of tangible property to which the owner has clear legal title.

In a sense the intangible assets of a business form a continuum which ranges, at one end, from the intangible but unequivocal rights which the business owns in such things as trade marks to, at the other, intangible assets which may be valuable and real but in which the company has no special title. These latter might include, for example, the fact that the chairman of a business plays golf with the chairman of another business: this might greatly benefit a business but is in no way an intangible asset to which the company can claim title.

The legal side of brands

Until a century or so ago business enterprises concerned themselves almost exclusively with tangible assets – plant, machinery, land and so on. It was only in the late nineteenth century that formal protection began to be afforded to trade marks and brands. Companies, therefore, had been mainly concerned with 'real' worth – factories, mines, ships and so forth. In attributing worth, though, to assets other than land businesses were already starting to take a substantial leap as until the nineteenth century the only asset which was considered to have any real worth was land.

In the last thirty years or so the recognition that intangibles have 'worth' has become more widespread. Indeed, most of the worth of many of today's leading corporations, ranging from Coca-Cola to IBM, is essentially intangible and the components which make up this worth include trade marks, designs, copyright in software, patents, etc. A considerable body of law now exists to protect intellectual property rights and because such rights lie at the core of brands, an understanding of their legal basis is essential to an understanding of brands.

Broadly, there are four main types of intellectual property. These are as follows:

1. *Patents* protect inventions. The inventor of a novel and non-obvious idea that is capable of industrial exploitation may be rewarded with a monopoly on that invention, normally for up to twenty years.
2. *Registered designs* relate to the features of shape, pattern, configuration and ornamentation of a useful article – for example, the distinctive shape of a piece of furniture, the pattern or motif on a set of crockery or the visual appeal of a woven fabric or of a wallpaper. Such designs can normally be protected for up to three consecutive five year periods.
3. *Copyright* applies to artistic, literary, dramatic and musical works. Normally one does not need to register copyright; it exists as soon as the 'product' comes out of the end of your pen or brush. (The exception is the United States where it is necessary to register copyright.) However, in order to enforce your rights you have to be able to prove that such rights do in fact exist and that they have been infringed. It is therefore essential to retain all the original material such as drawings and drafts in which copyright might reside.

124

Copyright protection generally extends from the time the work is created to 50 years after the death of the author or originator.

4. *Trade marks* are words or symbols that are used to distinguish the products or services of one manufacturer or supplier from those of another. By registering a trade mark, a supplier can obtain, in that country, a monopoly of his trade mark in relation to specified goods or services. The period of this monopoly can be unlimited, provided the registration is renewed and otherwise properly maintained.

By way of example, Kodak is a trade mark of Eastman Kodak Corporation. The brand name is protected internationally through trade mark registration. No doubt certain of the machines used in the manufacture of Kodak film are protected by patents. Certain features of the design of the product or of its packaging will, undoubtedly, be protected by registered designs. The distinctive logo design, as well as being in all probability a registered trade mark, will also be protected by copyright. The advertising material used in the promotion of the product, the technical manuals, original drawings, and so forth will all also be protected by copyright.

Brand owners can therefore use a complex of different intellectual property rights in order to protect their brands. Recently, for example, Jordache, a major American jeans manufacturer, suffered massive counterfeiting problems in Venezuela but was unable to use its Venezuelan trade mark registration to stop the counterfeiting as it proved to be invalid – a local company had got there first. However, it was able to show that it owned copyright in the distinctive stallion's head logo, and since Venezuela had signed an international treaty which provided protection for copyright holders, the logo was able to be used to stop the counterfeiting. In practice, however, the most potent legal right so far as most brands are concerned is the trade mark.

Most companies now recognise the value of their trade marks and protect them carefully, but this approach is by no means universal. It is still quite common for companies to lose their trade mark rights in one country or another because they have failed to register them or guard them sufficiently carefully. This chapter explains what a trade mark is, its function, the registration process, advantages of registration and how trade marks can be bought, sold or licensed. It focuses mainly on the

The legal side of brands

British trade mark law system though the same broad principles of trade mark law apply around the world.

Functions of a trade mark

In law, the functions of a trade mark are threefold:

1. To distinguish the goods or services of an enterprise from those of others.
2. To indicate the source or origin of the goods or services.
3. To represent the goodwill of the trade mark owner and to serve as an indication of the quality of his or her goods or services.

A trade mark can be a word or words, letters, numbers, symbols, emblems, drawings, pictures, monograms, signatures, colours or combinations of colours or any combination of these individual elements. In some cases a trade mark can be a phrase or slogan. The term 'trade mark' also includes what are often referred to as brand names and trade names. In many instances a company name can also function as a trade mark.

Registering a trade mark

Set out in the appendix is a more-or-less random sample of the several hundred trade marks advertised prior to registration in the official UK *Trade Marks Journal* of 9 August 1989, published by the Patent Office. This journal is published weekly and contains details of those trade marks which have passed an initial screening process but which have not yet obtained registration; publication provides an opportunity for objections to be raised by third parties prior to formal registration. It can be seen from this sample of trade mark applications that they cover words, symbols and almost every variation thereof. It also illustrates the range of companies seeking trade mark protection, their geographical spread and the rich opportunities for disputes and disagreements to arise, however ill-founded. This selection also shows examples of applications by brand owners seeking protection across a number of different classes, presumably for licensing purposes (e.g. Miami Dolphins); of brand owners who are seeking to extend the scope of protection into other classes of goods or services, presumably mainly for defensive purposes

126

(e.g. Pepsi) and of brand owners seeking to register trade marks modelled on a language clearly not that of the country of origin of the goods – a practice which at times has provoked a measure of trade mark 'nationalism' (e.g. Xi'a Xi'ang).

In the United Kingdom and other common law countries such as the United States and Australia, rights in a trade mark are acquired primarily through use rather than registration and the owner of a mark, whether it is registered or not can object to use of the same or similar mark on the grounds that such use amounts to 'passing off'. Some three hundred years ago it was held in an English Court that, 'nobody has the right to represent his goods as the goods of somebody else' and this is still valid today. In fact, the first formal registration system for trade marks was started in the sixteenth century by the Sheffield cutlery manufacturers to control the use of marks on knives and other cutlery in the Sheffield area. The first Act in the United Kingdom to provide for trade mark registration for all kinds of goods was in 1875; this has been successively replaced since then. The current Act is the Trade Marks Act, 1938, which was amended by the 1984 Act which introduced service mark registration – until 1984 registered trade marks in the United Kingdom covered only goods and not services.

The purpose of registration is to provide the owner of a trade mark with a statutory monopoly in the mark for the goods or services covered by the registration. Through an action in the High Court for trade mark infringement, the owner has the right to prevent the unauthorised use of the same or a confusingly similar mark on any of the goods or services covered by his registration. If the infringement action is successful the trade mark owner will be entitled to an injunction preventing the infringer from continuing to use the mark as well as an award of damages and the legal costs of bringing the action.

Registration of trade marks is not, however, compulsory and, as already mentioned, in the United Kingdom and other common law countries a trader can rely on an action for 'passing off' to protect his or her mark. However, registering a trade mark has important advantages:

1. To succeed in an action for passing off, the plaintiff has to establish to the court's satisfaction that he or she has a reputation and goodwill in his or her trade mark and that what the defendant is doing amounts to a misrepresentation which is confusing or likely to

confuse a substantial number of people into thinking that the defendant's goods or services come from the plaintiff, thereby causing damage to the plaintiff's business. Common law rights are therefore difficult, time consuming and expensive to establish and enforce, and the outcome of legal actions involving common law rights is frequently unpredictable. By contrast, to succeed in an action for trade mark infringement, the trade mark owner merely has to establish that his registration is valid and that the defendant is using the same or a confusingly similar mark on goods or services covered by his registration. The rights acquired through registration are therefore relatively simple and inexpensive to enforce and the outcome of infringement actions is generally much more certain and much less expensive.

2. In the United Kingdom and most other countries it is not necessary for a trade mark owner to be using his mark before he applies for registration. Thus an application can be filed for registration based on a genuine intention to use the mark in the future. This means that the mark can be protected before the product or service on which it is to be used has been launched. Common law rights in an unregistered mark, on the other hand, only arise through use over a period of time (often quite extended) and the owner of the unregistered mark clearly runs the risk of a third party entering the market before sufficient use has been made of the mark for it to enjoy any protection.

3. The owner or registered user of a trade mark registration can prevent the importation of infringing goods by lodging a notice with the Customs and Excise authorities.

4. In countries where there is no common law system (and this includes much of Continental Europe) rights in a trade mark are acquired mainly by registration not use. Registration may, in such countries, be the only option if the brand owner wants to enjoy any strong protection in his or her trade mark although, in certain circumstances, unfair competition laws can give a measure of protection.

5. A trade mark registration acts as a powerful deterrent to competitors considering the adoption of the same or similar mark because most manufacturers and traders carry out availability searches of the relevant trade mark registers before adopting a new mark so as to ensure that it does not conflict with existing third party rights.

128

Moreover, any infringer is more likely to be persuaded to back down when faced with an existing trade mark registration than with claimed common law rights.

Criteria for registrability

The criteria for registrability of a trade mark differ substantially from country to country. The United Kingdom has a fairly stringent system which includes examination of a mark for inherent registrability and for conflict with prior registered and pending marks before registration is granted. The American system is similar though less stringent. To qualify for registration in the United Kingdom, a new trade mark should not be deceptive or scandalous and should consist of or contain one or more of the following elements:

1. An invented word or words.
2. A word or words having no directly descriptive meaning in relation to the goods or services applied for, and not consisting of surnames or geographical names.
3. The name of a company or individual represented in a distinctive way.
4. The signature of the applicant or one of his or her predecessors in the business.
5. Any other distinctive mark such as a device or logo.

Generally, the most important factor in selecting a trade mark is *distinctiveness* – the trade mark should stand out from the crowd and unequivocally distinguish your goods or services. It is, however, sometimes possible to obtain registration of a mark which would not otherwise qualify for registration by providing evidence to show that the mark has been used for the goods or services covered by the application over a number of years prior to the date of application. The rationale for this is that the mark may have become distinctive through use and should therefore qualify for registration on these grounds. An example of such a mark would be Guinness for stout and related products. In theory, there might be many people called Guinness or McGuinness who might wish to brew beer and sell it under their own names; in practice, the name Guinness has become so indelibly linked with the particular products of the Arthur Guinness Brewery that it is entirely appropriate that Guinness should be awarded exclusive rights in the name in spite of the fact it is a relatively common surname.

Selecting a trade mark

From a trade mark owner's point of view the most attractive mark is often thought to be one which best describes his goods or services (e.g. owners and their advertising agencies are often drawn inexorably towards laudatory descriptors such as Supacote for paint or Easipic for instant photography). However, from a legal viewpoint the strongest type of trade mark is normally one which consists of an invented word, because such marks are much more readily registered and protected on an international basis. Moreover, as such 'invented' trade marks are quite clearly and unequivocally invented (they are not, for example, mere modifications of words frequently used in relation to the product), they are much more readily defended as pieces of intellectual property and are afforded much more deference by the courts. Examples of well known invented trade marks include Kodak, Oxo and Xerox.

Before adopting a new mark it is always advisable to carry out searches of the trade mark registers of the relevant countries to ensure that the mark does not conflict with existing third party rights. Although a search in one country is usually quick and inexpensive, it is far more difficult, time consuming and costly to clear a mark for international use, especially for such goods as pharmaceuticals or computers where the registers are already very crowded. Indeed, it is estimated that the world's trade mark registers now contain some twenty-five million marks and that the numbers will double by the end of the century. Europe alone has well over four million registered trade marks, Japan three million and the United States some two million. Clearly, finding a trade mark which is clear on an international basis is becoming extremely difficult and searching is essential to ensure that the launch of a new product or service will not give rise to third party objections or even infringement proceedings.

In the United Kingdom and other common law countries where rights can exist without registration it is also sensible to carry out additional searches of the index of company names and of relevant trade and telephone directories to ensure as far as possible that there are no potential problems from unregistered marks.

The process of registration

Once a mark has been cleared in the applicant's home country it is sensible to apply immediately for registration in order to lay claim to the mark pending completion of the international searches. It is possible to do this because, in many countries, once an application has been filed in one's home country, the applicant then has six months within which to file corresponding applications in other countries, claiming the filing date of the first country. This process gives the applicant priority over any conflicting applications filed in the intervening period. Of course, if you decide as a result of the international searches not to proceed with the mark you simply withdraw your home country application.

This initial six month period, which is ratified by international convention, can be extremely useful because it 'freezes' the position internationally for a period and gives the applicant time to complete the further searches, negotiate with the owners of any potentially conflicting prior marks, and to check whether apparently conflicting marks have in fact been used. (In many countries registrations can be cancelled on the grounds of five years' non-use.) In practice it is most unusual for international availability searches not to locate potential problems, at least in one or two countries. This is especially true of searches in more crowded product or service categories. However, it is often possible to overcome such problems by negotiating with the owner or owners of any conflicting marks who may be persuaded to restrict use of the mark to particular goods or services. Alternatively, it may be that the owner of the prior mark has lost interest and is prepared to assign his registration for a sum of money or that the validity of the conflicting mark can be challenged on the grounds of non-use.

The actual registration procedure differs quite considerably from country to country and ranges from a simple deposit system in countries such as France and Italy (i.e. a system where you merely stake a claim through registration but where the courts are left to sort out any problems) through to a system involving thorough examination both as to inherent registrability and conflict with prior marks before registration is granted. Such a system exists in the United Kingdom and America.

For the purpose of trade mark registration, goods and services are divided into forty-two classes known as the International Classification of Goods and Services. In the United Kingdom a separate application must be filed in each class for which protection is required, specifying the goods or services in that class for which the mark is to be used. Once the application has been filed, a filing receipt is issued by the Trade Marks Registry confirming the application date and number. This date is important because any rights eventually granted by registration are backdated to the original application date.

In the United Kingdom approximately one year after the application is filed it will be examined by the Registrar of Trade Marks to see whether the mark qualifies for registration (i.e. the Registrar checks that it is distinctive, that it is not merely descriptive and also that it is not deceptive, etc.). The Registrar also makes a check to ensure that it does not conflict with existing registrations or applications. If objections are raised on any of these grounds it is often possible to overcome them by arguing the case with the Registry or by submitting evidence to show that the mark has been used in the United Kingdom over a number of years prior to the date of application. Objections can sometimes also be overcome by amending the specification of goods or services covered by the application or by negotiating with the owners of conflicting prior marks.

Once the application has been accepted for registration in the United Kingdom it is advertised in the *Trade Marks Journal* so that any interested third parties can oppose it (see the appendix). Provided no oppositions are filed, the application then proceeds to registration on payment of the registration fee. For a reasonably straightforward application in the United Kingdom, the registration procedure is likely to take approximately two years to complete. Elsewhere, registration can take from six months to six years, and perhaps even longer in exceptional cases.

The cost of obtaining a trade mark registration in the United Kingdom averages about £600 per application, provided no serious problems are encountered. This sum would cover all official fees as well as the fees of a trade mark agent. The costs in other countries range from £300 to £2,000 or even more. Trade mark protection is therefore quite inexpensive to obtain while the rights conferred are powerful and extensive. However, when the mark is protected in two or three classes (it may be sensible, for example, to protect a trade mark for cough sweets in two classes: confectionery and pharmaceutical) or when more than one mark needs to be protected to cover a single brand (e.g. the name itself plus a logo) or when a number of countries are involved, then the actual number of trade mark registrations may be high and the costs of securing strong international protection for the brand can be substantial. An important international brand may thus be protected by dozens or even hundreds of individual trade marks registrations.

In the United Kingdom a trade mark registration lasts for seven years from the date of the original application and can then be renewed for further periods of fourteen years. The duration of overseas registrations varies from country to country but in many cases is ten years; in other words, the trade mark registrations need to be renewed every ten years. However, even if a registration has been renewed, in most countries it can be cancelled on the grounds of non-use, at the instigation of an interested third party, usually after five years. In some countries it is necessary to prove that a mark is being used before the registration will be renewed. In every country, a registration may be renewed indefinitely; unlike other forms of intellectual property such as patents and copyrights, trade marks have potentially an unlimited life provided they are properly used, properly renewed and otherwise cared for, e.g. guarded against infringement and counterfeiting.

Licensing

Licensing of trade marks occurs where the trade mark owner allows others to use his marks, often in return for a royalty or for other payments. United Kingdom trade mark law permits licensing, subject to certain conditions, and the licensee can be recorded on the register of trade marks as a 'registered user'. Use of a mark by a registered user is deemed to be use of the mark by the owner. However, the Registrar of Trade Marks will not allow a licensee to be registered as a registered user unless he is satisfied that use of the mark is controlled by the registered proprietor, either by being a subsidiary company or through a licence agreement. In particular, the registered proprietor is required to be able to control the quality of the goods or services sold under the trade mark so that the function of the mark as an indication of origin is not destroyed. Trade mark licensing is of particular importance to the fast-growing franchising industry, as it is the right to use the franchisor's mark which is often the most important element in the total package which the franchisee acquires.

Although the concept of licensing of trade marks is recognised in many countries, it is important for the licensor to comply with any local requirements to ensure that his or her registration is not invalidated. In particular, it is important to ensure that licensees do not come to regard the mark as their property rather than the licensor's. This is a very common problem for licensors and franchisors alike, as without a strong legal position they may find their case obstructed by local judges who, at times, appear for economic or political reasons to favour the local company.

Transferring ownership of a trade mark

In the United Kingdom as well as in many other countries the transfer of ownership of a trade mark registration can take place with or without the goodwill of the business in the goods or services for which the mark is registered. An assignment has to be executed by the assignor and an application filed at the Trade Marks Registry in order to have the transfer of ownership recorded on the register. An unregistered trade mark may also be assigned but usually only with the goodwill of the business.

Failure to record an assignment on the Trade Marks Register can lead to problems and delays if the new owner wishes to sue for trade mark infringement. It is therefore important to take appropriate steps to have assignments recorded as soon as possible.

Counterfeiting

One of the major problems facing many brand owners today is that of counterfeiting. In 1984 the US International Trade Commission put the losses suffered by American companies as a result of product counterfeiting at between $6 and $8 billion annually, and it seems clear that the figure has risen markedly since then. It is not just American companies, though, that suffer from counterfeiting; Louis Vuitton, the French manufacturer of luxury luggage and accessories, has estimated that some 92 per cent of all so-called Louis Vuitton luggage sold throughout the world is counterfeit, a problem which not only results in lost revenue but, equally importantly, debases the excellence and exclusivity of the genuine product.

Counterfeiting can also have profound implications for product quality and product safety. The Anti-counterfeiting Group, a British-based organisation comprising major manufacturing companies, has identified the following examples of 'safety critical' counterfeits seized over the last few years.

Counterfeit products	Comments
Brake shoes and linings	These are regularly copied and the brakes vary in quality from bad to lethal. One batch seized took ten times as long to stop a vehicle in an emergency stop as the genuine product. Another batch was made of compressed grass rather than friction material and burst into flames on test. Found in Nigeria.
Bus brake diaphragms	Counterfeit brake diaphragms to control the air brakes of public buses were found, luckily before any accident occurred. The copies burst on test after as few as eight applications. This would render the air brakes inoperative. Genuine performance standards specify over one million applications. Found in the United Kingdom.
Industrial hoists	Copy products failed to incorporate a vital safety brake. This could easily have caused death or injury. Found in Canada.
Nuts and bolts for the construction industry	Caused parts of a building to collapse during an earthquake. Found in the United States.
Hand tools	Made of steel so brittle that they broke into razor sharp fragments if used. Found in the United Kingdom.
Electric sockets	Inadequately insulated. Liable to blow up, cause electrocution or fires. Found in the Middle East.
Insecticide	Marked 'safe for use near food' but contents actually highly toxic. Found in the Middle East.
Fungicide	Destroyed an entire annual coffee crop. Found in Kenya.

Counterfeit products	Comments
Helicopter parts	Resulted in several accidents. The legitimate manufacturer faced a number of court actions as a result. Found in the United States.
Aircraft hydraulic brake parts	Leaked brake fluid causing several accidents. Found in the United States.
Aircraft brake parts	Made from mild steel rather than tempered steel. Found in the United Kingdom.
Ulcer drugs	Reports suggested 'little or no beneficial effect'. Found in the United Kingdom.
Eye drops	Contained no active ingredient but made with contaminated water. Could cause blindness if put into an infected eye. Found in Nigeria.
Antibiotics	Analysis showed made from vegetable matter and talcum powder. No active ingredients. Found in Africa.

Source: *Counterfeiting – How GATT can help*, published by the Anti-counterfeiting Group.

The products which suffer most from counterfeiting are those which have a high added value as a result of the 'intellectual property' inherent in the product. Besides engineered and pharmaceutical products, these include: fragrances (where the cost of producing the product is a small percentage of the selling price); audio tapes and videos; spirits, liqueurs, champagnes and wines; watches, handbags, luggage and other similar luxury items; high value consumable components such as needles for carpet tufting machines; and even valves for heart pumps.

Generally, counterfeiting arises for two main reasons. Firstly, in Third World countries counterfeiting frequently flourishes either because the country is starved of foreign exchange and cannot afford to buy 'luxury' items or because the citizens of those countries simply do not have the disposable income to afford the genuine product. Textbooks are routinely counterfeited in India; Thailand has a large and flourishing counterfeit music industry, and Brazil is awash with counterfeit Lacoste leisurewear, Paco Rabanne fragrances and Cartier watches. While, to some extent, counterfeiting under such circumstances is understandable, it can cause major problems and often is far from innocent. In 1978 much of Kenya's coffee crop was ruined when it was treated with useless, locally-produced counterfeit fungicide.

Secondly, and more insidiously, counterfeiting in the developed world has become a major activity of gangs involved in organised crime and who often have sophisticated manufacturing and distribution networks. The availability of technology such as offset printing machinery, computers and high speed video tape reproduction equipment has greatly aided the counterfeiter as formerly it would have been impossible in many instances to produce a plausible counterfeit at low cost without large investment. Now counterfeiters can set up production units quickly and cheaply and can, if detected, simply move on or treat the loss of any seized goods and equipment as merely an inevitable and acceptable business overhead.

Brand owners need to be vigilant and aggressive in protecting their rights. Until quite recently, legal systems in countries like Britain had not generally introduced stiff penalties to punish such crimes as piracy of computer software. Thus even though the courts would frequently sympathise with the brand or copyright owner whose rights had been infringed, the counterfeiter would be little concerned by the sanctions imposed. This is changing. In Britain, for example, counterfeiting has now become a criminal rather than a civil offence as a result of the Copyright, Designs and Patents Act, 1988, and the US government, through the GATT (General Agreement on Tariffs and Trade) negotiations, is encouraging all its trading partners to take a much tougher line on counterfeiting.

Although counterfeiters can infringe any or all of a brand owner's intellectual property rights, in practice it is trade mark rights which are most frequently infringed and which are the easiest and least expensive to defend.

The power of trade marks

Brands and trade marks are frequently seen as being hazy and insubstantial pieces of property. In fact, the rights attaching to them can be very powerful and every major country in the world has well-developed systems for their protection. The cost of establishing these rights is also relatively modest, particularly when compared with the costs of establishing and maintaining brands or even with the cost of patenting.

Perhaps most importantly, trade marks do not have finite life. Provided the trade mark owner maintains and renews his trade marks they can go on indefinitely and gain in value and power with investment and exposure in the marketplace. They are, therefore, fundamentally different from patents and other forms of intellectual property.

Trade marks are also quite complex, and care must be taken in their creation and management. It is all too easy, for example, to adopt a new mark with only very narrow protection, or with other legal defects or which is strictly limited in its geographical scope. Alternatively, it is easy for a mark to be damaged by poor brand or trade mark management or by adopting a too *laissez-faire* attitude towards, for example, the precise way in which the mark is used or towards counterfeiting.

Using the trade mark

A trade mark is a sign or symbol which distinguishes the goods or services of an enterprise. When using the trade mark it is important to ensure that this distinguishing function is preserved and that the trade mark does not become, for example, merely a generic name available to all-comers. (This has happened to such former trade marks as aspirin, kerosene, escalator, thermos and cellophane, at least in certain countries.)

It is important, therefore, to ensure that the trade mark is used correctly, particularly by the company's own employees and agents. The following rules, if consistently applied, should ensure that the company does not lose its trade mark rights.

Rule 1
Whenever your trade mark appears in print make sure that it stands out from the surrounding text. To do this, you should always capitalise the first letter of your trade mark and you may also use italics or bold print. (Conversely, you should treat the generic name as a normal word and not capitalise its first letter.)

Proper use: The Toshiba fax machine offers excellent value for money. Improper use: The toshiba fax machine offers excellent value for money.

Rule 2
Always follow the trade mark with the generic or dictionary name.

Proper use: Hovis flour contains wheatgerm.
Improper use: Hovis contains wheatgerm.

Rule 3
Always use your trade mark as an adjective, never as a noun; never pluralise your trade mark; never use it in the possessive; never use it as a verb.

Proper use: Apple computer's special features . . .
Improper use: Apple's special features . . .

Rule 4
Never fool about with the spelling of your trade mark.

Proper use: Twix bars last for ever!
Improper use: Twixxxxxxx bars last for ever!

Rule 5
Maintain a consistent visual identity for your trade mark; do not allow a proliferation of different graphic treatments.

Rule 6
Show the world that the word or symbol is in fact your trade mark and that you mean to keep it that way through the use of the appropriate symbol, ®, ™ or ℠. (The first normally refers to a registered trade mark, the second often indicates an unregistered trade mark and the last a service mark.)

The trade mark adviser

Trade marks are a quite complex and specialist area of law. It is well worth taking proper advice about selecting, registering, defending and using a trade mark.

15
Licensing and franchising

In the last twenty years there has been a rapid growth in brand licensing and franchising; indeed the latter activity is almost entirely a modern phenomenon though licensing, particularly of patents and technical know-how, has a much longer-established pedigree.

Licensing

Brand (or trade mark) licensing is the practice of allowing others to use one's brands on approved goods or services and in a way which allows the owner to control the quality of the goods or services covered by the licence. It takes three main forms: the first is the licensing of third parties to produce or offer to supply more-or-less the same goods or services as those produced by the brand owner. Usually such licences are granted in countries where the brand owner does not operate. Kingfisher, for example, an Indian brand of beer, is produced under licence in Britain by a licensee acting under the authority of the Indian owner of the trade mark.

The goods covered by the licence, and their quality should be strictly controlled by the licensor. Often the licensee is an independent third party and the licensor and the licensee have no relationship other than through the brand which they both exploit in their separate markets to their mutual benefit. Often, however, the licensee will be a subsidiary of the brand owner but, as the brands are owned by the parent and not the subsidiary, the subsidiary is formally a licensed user of the trade marks. Increasingly, brand owners require their subsidiaries to pay the same fees for the use of any such licensed brands as they would charge to a third party because in this way the value of the assets being licensed is fully recognised. Also, in certain circumstances, particularly when tax rates are lower in the country where the parent is based than in the country where the subsidiary is located, this type of internal brand licensing can be highly tax efficient.

A second form of brand licensing, referred to in the United States as 'collateral exploitation', is the practice of licensing well-known trade marks for use on goods and services unrelated to those goods or services for which the trade mark originally achieved fame. The reason why owners of famous trade marks allow collateral exploitation is partly financial – the licence revenues can be substantial, are largely risk-free and may require little effort on the part of the brand owner – and partly because such trade mark licensing enhances the trade mark strength, broadens the line of products on which the marks are used and hence, where the company has established trade mark rights, results in greater trade mark exposure and results in a highly interested network of licensees to monitor and report any trade mark infringements by unauthorised third parties.

Coca-Cola, for example, licensed Murjani, an American-based clothing company originally known for its highly successful exploitation of the Gloria Vanderbilt range of jeans, to produce a range of Coca-Cola brand sportswear. The range proved highly successful and the royalty income to Coca-Cola was substantial. Perhaps more importantly, millions of consumers voluntarily turned themselves into mobile billboards to promote the Coca-Cola name and logo; indeed, they paid to do so.

Rolls-Royce also pursues a licensing policy, but for quite different reasons. Rolls-Royce has constant and serious problems of misuse of its trade marks by third parties. Around the world the name Rolls-Royce has become so synonymous with excellence, leadership, style and sophistication that producers of all sorts of goods and services reckon that if they can expropriate the Rolls-Royce name and logo and use it on their own goods and services they can impart to them all the favourable associations of the Rolls-Royce name. The infringements which Rolls-Royce suffers range from coy references to blatant counterfeiting. Numerous car converters, for example, have taken every conceivable model of car from Austins to Chevrolets and have converted them into

'Rolls-Royces' through the addition of a grill, a model of 'The Spirit of Ecstasy' and suitable Rolls-Royce insignia on hub cap and boot lids. In addition, every conceivable type of 'Rolls-Royce' product or service has been marketed without authority at one time or another including fragrances, fashion accessories, night clubs, luggage, even dental chairs. Indeed, the practice of advertising a product as 'the Rolls-Royce of plastic extruders', or some such, has become at times almost endemic.

Rolls-Royce is not without a sense of humour and tries not to be too heavy-handed. It recognises, however, that it is the company's responsibility both to its shareholders and to Rolls-Royce owners to maintain the exclusivity of the brand and ensure that it does not become abused or, *in extremis*, a laughing stock. They have therefore instituted a system of controlled collateral licensing whereby a carefully selected licensee is appointed in each product sector and is required to produce goods of exclusivity and high quality. The scope of such exploitation is quite limited and the licence income is modest but it provides Rolls-Royce with a unique, highly informed and highly motivated monitoring system which locates infringements at an early stage and allows Rolls-Royce to deal with them before they have developed too far. In addition, Rolls-Royce advertises regularly in leading trade journals such as *Trademark World* to alert trade mark attorneys around the world as to their strong interest in protecting their trade marks. (A typical such advertisement is shown in Figure 15.1.)

The third main form of licensing is the successful commercial practice known as character merchandising. This form of trade mark exploitation was originally pioneered by the owners of successful Hollywood movie properties such as the Walt Disney characters, Kojak, ET and so on. Such characters may only enjoy a relatively short commercial career so if the enormous costs of producing the movie are not recovered in a few months then they will never be. By licensing the use of these popular movie characters on toys, games, T-shirts, video games, soaps, confectionery products, etc. a lucrative new source of income can be exploited.

More recently, this form of merchandising has been further developed by brand owners who have no connection with the entertainment industry. The Strawberry Shortcake character, for example, was developed by the American Greetings Corporation specifically for

Rolls-Royce

This is NOT a good name for your
New Restaurant

Nor is it the way to describe
THE BEST GARDEN SPADE
ON THE MARKET

Nor can this be the eye-catching sign
for your new wedding car service.

The name ROLLS-ROYCE, the ROLLS-RR-
ROYCE badge and the interlocking RR logo,
belong to Rolls-Royce PLC and are the subject of
comprehensive trade mark registrations in 96
countries.

They are used under exclusive licence for
motor cars by Rolls-Royce Motor Cars Limited,
who also have registrations for their distinctive
Palladian Radiator Grille and Flying Lady
mascot, not to mention a lot of model titles.

We are always interested to hear of any misuse
of our name from our colleagues in the trade
mark world.

Rolls-Royce PLC
PO Box 31
Derby DE2 8BJ

Rolls-Royce Motor Cars Ltd
Crewe
Cheshire CW1 3PL

Figure 15.1 A Rolls-Royce press advertisement indicating the
company's constant vigilance towards its trade marks

merchandising purposes and is now licensed for use on such items as
lunch boxes, greetings cards, dolls and other toys.

Franchising

Franchising is concerned with the granting of rights to a number
(frequently large) of different licensees in different geographical areas.
Usually the rights being licensed are not just intellectual property rights
such as trade marks and logos but are in effect, the right to copy the

franchisor's successful business concept down to the smallest detail. Thus franchise agreements often cover the look and design of the business, the uniforms of employees, promotional materials, and so forth. In addition, the benefits provided by the franchisor frequently include staff training, specialised accountancy and business control systems, computer software, assistance with staff selection and so on; indeed, every possible type of assistance that a person might need to establish and manage a successful business.

The franchisor therefore provides to the franchisee a great deal of proprietary business information and material besides the right to use the trade mark, though the trade mark is of core importance and is often the feature which, in legal terms, most firmly binds the relationship together. After all, once a franchise is successfully established the franchisor can hardly take back his know-how but if the franchisee fails to pay the licence fee, operate the franchise in the approved fashion or if he terminates or breaks the franchise agreement for some other reason the franchisor can and will withdraw the right to use his other trade marks, copyright and other intellectual property rights.

McDonald's fast food restaurants are probably the most successful and best-known franchise in the world, and it is largely this company's success which has stimulated the massive growth in many different franchise businesses around the world. Franchises have proved, generally, to be particularly successful in the fast food and retail areas as such enterprises benefit greatly from being part of a national or international chain yet require the close attention, dedication and entrepreneurial drive of a sole proprietor to make them successful. Franchising is, therefore, often a tailor-made solution in such sectors. It is, however, a tenet of the franchise industry that there is no commercial activity which cannot be franchised. In Australia, for example, the second largest supplier of homes (soon, most likely, the largest), Nu-Steel, is a franchise – the company has developed a system whereby a prospective home-owner visits a Nu-Steel franchise, specifies a home and Nu-Steel fabricates the frame of the home in steel to the customer's specification. The owner-builder then arranges for the frame to be erected and adds windows, doors, a roof, cladding, internal finishes, etc. All these components are available in great variety and to a high specification, and owner-builders can construct their own franchised home for around 20 per cent less than it costs to buy a house conventionally. Successful franchises also exist for drain cleaning (e.g. Dyno-Rod in the United Kingdom), termite control, roofing systems, etc. In California there is even a franchised service whereby the franchisee periodically visits hotels with a specially equipped vehicle and cleans and restuffs hotel pillows.

The franchise industry is now a huge and mature one with very considerable accumulated experience. One of the inevitable features of the industry is the 'tension' which exists between franchisor and franchisee – the franchisee is selected (or self-selected) for his or her entrepreneurialism and drive yet, at the same time, the franchisor requires the franchisee to operate according to strict rules and regulations. Not surprisingly, the franchisor often thinks of the franchisees as ungrateful, spoiled and opinionated and the franchisee often considers the franchisor to be arrogant and unbending. In many franchises relationships can become quite strained and it is often the oldest, most experienced and most successful franchisees who take the greatest pleasure in acting as the stag of the herd and clashing horns with the franchisor.

Those experienced in the franchise industry tend to regard this tension as inevitable, and it is clear that a strong brand name and unequivocal legal rights to the brand name are often the key features in holding franchises together. 'If it wasn't for the fact that I'd have to give up using the brand name I'd have no hesitation in telling them where to go when the franchise comes up for renewal'. The power of the brand and the importance of strong legal rights are nowhere better illustrated than in the franchise area.

Legal aspects

In both brand licensing and franchising it is essential to ensure that the brand is protected by registration for all those goods and countries where rights are to be licensed. Most countries do not, in fact, recognise licensing of trade marks for goods or services unless there is a trade mark registration, but even where they do it is a highly risky procedure. It is also sensible to record the licensee as a registered user as this avoids the possibility of cancellation proceedings against the proprietor on the grounds of non-use; it also makes the licence a matter of public record.

Furthermore, since in law a trade mark indicates the source or origin of the goods or services it is essential that the trade mark owner controls the nature and quality of the goods or services covered by the licence so that the concept of identification of source is maintained. In order that the licensor's rights are protected it is also essential that any licence agreement is carefully drafted and covers some or all of the following points:

1. The trade mark, together with the goods or services covered by the licence, should be clearly identified along with details of trade mark registrations, specific exclusions or limitations and so forth.
2. The nature of the licence should be specified – sole, exclusive, non-exclusive, etc. (A sole licence extends to the licensee and no one else but does not preclude the licensor from using the mark; an exclusive licence would normally exclude even the licensor from using the mark on the goods or services which are being licensed.)
3. Indemnification provisions whereby the licensee indemnifies the licensor from damages caused by a licensed product.
4. Territorial limitations.
5. Provisions for quality control and how such control will be enforced.
6. Specific acknowledgement by the licensee of the licensor's title together with an agreement that the benefit of use will flow to the licensor and that the licensee will take no actions prejudicial to the licensor's interest in or ownership of the trade mark or marks.
7. Specific provisions for termination, for example in the case of non-compliance. The licence should also have provisions for seeking to cure any default through the serving of notices but, in the event of termination, the rights of the licensor and the licensee should be clear. In particular, there should be an immediate cessation of all use of the mark by the licensee together with a requirement that the licensee surrenders to the licensor all goods bearing the licensed mark, perhaps at an agreed price (e.g. cost price). In certain instances the licensee or franchisee may be required also to surrender other valuable rights, for example a location.
8. Specific provisions as to how the trade mark may be used – colour, typeface dimension, etc. In addition, the licensor may require that, wherever the mark is used, there is an acknowledgement or an identification as to ownership, e.g. 'Mark is trade mark of ABC Company' or 'Mark owned by and used under licence from ABC Company'.

Just as the consequences of making a wrong decision about a new trade mark can be profound so too can be the consequences of lax licensing or franchising. Over time it is easy for licensees to come to regard the mark as their property despite knowing, in a sense, that they are not the real owners. Nonetheless, licensees or franchisees often argue that it is they who have developed the market or the franchise from nothing and it is they who risked their capital in doing so; really, therefore, by any interpretation they deserve to own the mark, not the licensor or franchisor. Although situations of this type by no means arise in all licences or franchises, strong legal rights and well-drafted agreements are essential for the avoidance of problems. It should also be remembered that in very many licences, especially technical licences, the bulk of the know-how is passed over in the first few months; if you wish your licensee to renew the licence and continue paying royalties once the licence expires in, say, ten years time, the key factor which may persuade him or her to do so is the right to continue to use the trade mark in which he or she has invested so much money and effort.

Conclusions

The growth of licensing and franchising activity around the world is staggering; in 1979 retail sales of licensed branded goods in America were $6.5 billion, by 1985 this figure had risen to $40 billion. In Japan the growth of licensing is even more marked. The Japanese have a fascination for Western brands, particularly those in the areas of fashion and luxury goods, and are willing to pay a substantial premium for goods bearing suitable Western brand names. In the light of the difficulties that Western manufacturers have in exporting to Japan and, in particular, in securing distribution in that country, the granting of licences to allow local manufacture is often the preferred solution.

The proportion of major brand owners now pursuing brand licensing strategies is high. In the United States, for example, Harley-Davidson, a company mainly known for its motorbikes, has licensed its brand for use on mugs, motor oil, clothing, cologne, leather jackets, even gold rings. Anheuser-Busch, the massive St Louis-based brewers, license the brand names Budweiser, Busch and Bud Light for beach towels, clothes, mugs, umbrellas, basketball backboards, lamps, coolers, inflatable human size beer cans, wallets, blankets, electric guitars and fishing lures. The owners of the Louisville Slugger brand of baseball bats now license the brand for use on children's wear and it is even possible to purchase in America Baryshnikov leisure and exercise wear, licensed by the ballet star himself.

Licensing and franchising are both strategies that any brand owner should consider to make his brands work harder for him and to increase their power and exposure in the marketplace. Like everything else, there are risks involved in doing so but, with care, these can be avoided and the rewards can be substantial.

16
Valuing brands

In 1984, News Group, the Australian flagship company of Rupert Murdoch's worldwide publishing empire, included a valuation for 'publishing titles' in its balance sheet. Murdoch did this because the 'goodwill' element of publishing acquisitions – the difference between the value of the net assets and the price paid – can be enormous and, being an acquisitive company, the goodwill write-offs which his company was being forced to take were ravaging his balance sheet. He knew well that much of the 'goodwill' he was buying comprised the publishing titles; he therefore placed a value on these and included this valuation in the balance sheet. This simple procedure restored his balance sheet, solved many of the problems of goodwill write-offs and dramatically reduced gearing. Indeed, without this balance sheet valuation of publishing titles it is unlikely that Murdoch would have been able to expand his business by acquisition, particularly in the United States.

Reckitt and Colman, the major British-based branded goods company with powerful brands in the toiletries, household products and foods sector was faced with exactly the same problem in 1985 having acquired Airwick Industries from Ciba-Geigy. It capitalised the value of the Airwick brand for if it had not done so its net assets would have been reduced considerably.

Next in line was the mighty Grand Met. In 1987 this company acquired Heublein, whose main asset was the Smirnoff brand. In August 1988 Grand Met announced that a large part of the sum paid for Heublein was attributable to the Smirnoff brand and would therefore not be written off but, rather, would be included as an acquired brand in its balance sheet at a sum of £588 million. Not until later in the year did observers realise that this move was a trailer to the massive $5.5 billion Pillsbury bid, successfully concluded in January 1989.

The News Group, Reckitt and Colman, and Grand Met brand valuations and other valuations in the publishing industry went largely unremarked upon. (Observers did not altogether realise that publishing titles are in fact brands.) However, what really put the cat among the accounting pigeons was the decision of Ranks Hovis McDougall plc (RHM), Britain's major flour and foods company, to value all its brands, acquired or otherwise, and to place this valuation in its balance sheet. News of this valuation broke in late November 1988 and the debate has raged ever since. This valuation was conducted in conjunction with Interbrand Group plc, the specialist international branding consultancy.

Since RHM valued its brands many major British quoted companies, including Guinness, United Biscuits and Lonrho, have included brand valuations in their balance sheets though mainly for acquired brands only – Guinness, for example, announced a £1.7 billion valuation of brands acquired in the previous four years. Many more companies, however, have valued their brands but not used the valuations for balance sheet purposes. Rather, they have been more concerned with brand management, strategy, brand licensing and with the valuation of brands for merger and acquisition purposes.

The phenomenon of brand valuation has also spread way beyond just Britain and Australia. An American observer, for example, remarked that, 'getting to grips with the value of important intangibles such as brands is one of the major challenges for US businesses and accountants in the 1990s'. Even Japanese business is taking an interest – overseas acquisitions by Japanese companies are increasingly taking place in the branded goods field where much of the acquired value is intangible. Japanese companies are as keen as any others to evaluate the worth of the intangible assets they are acquiring.

The brand valuation controversy

Much of the impetus for brand valuation in Britain and Australia has stemmed from a desire by companies with weakened balance sheets as a result of goodwill write-offs following acquisitions to restore the strength of their balance sheets by including a figure to reflect the value of their intangible brand assets. (In the United States, accounting principles do not allow the revaluation of assets for balance sheet purposes, so the 'brands on the balance sheet' debate has largely passed them by. However, brand valuation is of increasing interest for planning mergers and acquisitions.)

Although the applications for brand valuation have grown substantially and now include mergers and acquisitions, brand management, brand licensing and fund raising, the 'balance sheet/brand valuation' debate continues, with interested parties on all sides contributing to it. Views on the subject are many. Accountancy firms are concerned that valuing brands is an imprecise exercise and that the introduction of value accounting threatens the fundamentals of historic cost accounting. Accountants in industry are delighted at the belated recognition being given to what many believe are the most important of corporate assets. The academic world has warned of the dangers of abandoning traditional accounting theory yet has offered no alternative solution. Financial journalists, recognising not only the rationale for a consistent approach to the issue of brand valuation but also a long overdue need to review the totality of financial accounting, have demanded action from the profession to produce relevant and realistic statements of accounting practice. Corporate boardrooms are frustrated by the inequity of seeing balance sheets eroded through goodwill write-offs and consequently welcome any development that enables corporate assets to be more fairly represented. The City seems content to remain somewhat distanced from the debate although the Stock Exchange has pronounced that brands should be recognised for purposes of establishing the underlying worth of companies. Adventurous bankers are starting to talk about issuing brand-backed securities and/or using brand collateral as security for debt issues. Shareholders, meanwhile, for whose protection balance sheets are prepared, seem quite happy to sit on the sidelines.

The significance of brand valuation

The 'balance sheet/brand valuation' debate is, however, not really about brands at all: it is about the role of accounting (how accounting should adapt to a changing business environment, especially one in which

Valuing brands

'worth' often principally comprises intangible, rather than tangible, assets) and the role of the balance sheet. The brand valuation debate has, therefore, precipitated a close look at issues which, many observers believe, the accountancy profession has fudged for far too long.

In many respects, therefore, the debate is something of a technical sideshow. Whatever accountants decide about the balance sheet, brand owners are aware that their brands are valuable and important. Investors and predators share precisely the same view.

While the balance sheet debate has raged, brand valuation has, more quietly, been applied in a number of quite different areas:

1. In mergers and acquisitions, particularly to identify and evaluate opportunities but also in disposals.
2. In brand licensing, both internally and to third parties. (This issue is discussed in the previous chapter.)
3. In fund raising. Brands are increasingly being used as collateral on loans as they are freely transferable assets with clear title confirmed by trade mark registration certificates. Brands are also starting to be the subject of sale and leaseback arrangements which are proving highly tax-efficient.
4. For brand management purposes. Brand evaluation and valuation techniques must necessarily be extremely methodical, highly analytical and very thorough. Such techniques analyse each brand's strengths and weaknesses and have proved to be a management tool of considerable importance and value, particularly in the areas of resource allocation, brand strategy development and performance tracking.

It seems quite certain that the major long-term impact of brand valuation will be in these areas rather than in the specialist area of balance sheet repair.

The development of brand awareness in mergers and acquisitions

The fact that brands are valuable assets has been fully recognised by predators and investors, especially following the Nestlé takeover of Rowntree in April 1988. In this case, a company with tangible net assets of around £300 million and a pre-bid capitalisation of around £1 billion was bought finally by Nestlé, who competed vigorously with Jacobs–

Suchard for the prize, for £2.5 billion. This event has jolted into action not only stock markets, but also those companies with a less-developed awareness of brand values. Thus we have seen an increased consciousness among investors of the potential value of brands with, in some cases, a reappraisal of the worth of companies with exceptional portfolios of strong brands. Equally, many companies have made a major push to increase investor awareness of the quality (and therefore worth) of their brand portfolios.

Consumer products companies know that it normally takes many years to establish a successful branded product, and that successful branded products have to cover the considerable costs of the majority of brands that fail. The investment required to establish a successful brand will have taken place over an extended period and will have been accounted for in a variety of ways – capitalised manufacturing plant, expensed or deferred R&D, expensed advertising and management costs, and so on – little of which will be separately identifiable in a company's accounts.

Until recently no attempt has been made in the mergers and acquisitions arena to revisit the issue of valuing intangibles. Stock markets and investment banks have been generally content to let any premium paid to net tangible assets fall into the nebulous accounting category of goodwill.

Changes in the perception and financial treatment of this premium to tangible assets have, however, started. This development has arisen for both conceptual and technical reasons. Conceptually, many companies have found it increasingly unacceptable that their balance sheets should show little indication of the true value of the company. Technically, the erosion of balance sheets by the conventional requirement to write off goodwill on acquisitions has left some companies looking over-geared. In addition, the current rules on goodwill accounting result in a peculiar anomaly: the more acquisitive a company is in the branded goods area (where it is axiomatic that the main asset one is buying is intangible), the more that company will be forced to take goodwill write-offs to reserves thus depleting net assets. Taken to its extreme a company such as Grand Metropolitan may find that its highly successful acquisition policy results in a balance sheet which owns no reserves at all, yet Grand Met owns one of the world's most powerful and valuable brand portfolios.

It is clear not only that this disparity between reality and accounting fiction is inappropriate but also that the Accounting Standards Committee should fulfil a responsibility to create and maintain a meaningful accounting system.

The RHM brand valuation

The change in the perception and financial treatment of brand values by companies active in mergers and acquisitions is well illustrated by the example of Ranks Hovis McDougall. The background to this pioneering step is instructive. Goodman Fielder Wattie, the Australian foods group, acquired a 15 per cent stake in RHM in 1986 from S. & W. Berisford and in 1988 bid for RHM on a prospective multiple of 15.5 times earnings. This bid was referred to the Monopolies and Mergers Commission and eventually lapsed. However, following the referral of the bid to the Commission the predator was left with a hostile 29.9 per cent stake with observers keenly anticipating the next move. The publication of the independent brand valuation conducted for RHM by Interbrand led to a concentration of interest on the importance of brands by stock markets, analysts and investment bankers.

The aggregate of RHM's net tangible assets following the brand valuation amounted to £0.98 billion, against the £1.78 billion price tag of the Goodman Fielder Wattie bid. The brand valuation was clearly not intended, therefore, to represent the worth of the business on a takeover. But what was it intended to represent? The answer is found in the text of RHM's own 1988 accounts:

> [The brand valuation] recognises the value of the brands as they are currently used by the Group and does not take account of their future prospects or, indeed, their worth in the open market.

RHM is not, of course, the only instance where brand valuation has been centre-stage during a takeover. The concept of brand value has featured prominently in a significant number of takeovers in recent years (see Table 16.1). Surprisingly, most of these takeovers required a large premium in order to secure victory. Surprisingly, because it might be reasonable to have expected the increasing number of takeovers in the food and drinks sector to have led stock markets to two conclusions:

1. A major restructuring of the global food and drink manufacturing industry was under way as companies attempted to achieve sufficient

The RHM brand valuation

Table 16.1   Recent brand acquisitions in the food and drinks sector

Purchaser	Company acquired	Some key brands acquired	Cost	Date
R. J. Reynolds	Nabisco	Ritz crackers, Planters nuts	$4.93bn	June 1985
Guinness	Arthur Bell	Bell's whisky	£365m	Aug. 1985
Philip Morris	General Foods	Bird's Eye, Maxwell House, Sanka	$5.8bn	Sept. 1985
Guinness	Distillers	Johnnie Walker, White Horse, Gordon's gin, Pimms	£2.7bn	April 1986
Allied Lyons	Hiram Walker	Canadian Club, Courvoisier cognac	£400m	Sept. 1986
Elders IXL	Courage	Courage beers	£1.4bn	Nov. 1986
Hillsdown Holdings	Maple Leaf Mills	Sun Maid raisins, Monarch flour, Purity flour	$169m	July 1987
Douwe Egberts	Akzo Consumer Products Division	Temana, Heidelberg, etc.	$612m	Sept. 1987
Cadbury Schweppes	Chocolat Poulain	Poulain chocolate	£94.3m	Dec. 1987
Seagram	Martell	Martell cognac	£525m	Feb. 1988
United Biscuits	Ross Young	Ross foods, Young's seafoods	£335m	Feb. 1988
Nestlé	Rowntree	Kit-Kat, Rolo, Quality Street	£2.5bn	April 1988
KKR	RJR Nabisco	Winston, Camel, Benson and Hedges, Nabisco	$25.3bn	Nov. 1988
Grand Metropolitan	Pillsbury	Pillsbury, Green Giant, Burger King	$5.23bn	Oct. 1988
Ranks Hovis McDougall	RJR Nabisco (Breakfast Cereals, UK)	Shredded Wheat, Shreddies, Team	£80m	Nov. 1988
Brent Walker	Whyte & Mackay	Whyte & Mackay	£180m	Nov. 1988
Cadbury Schweppes	Bassett foods	Liquorice Allsorts, Jelly Babies, Dolly Mixtures	£86m	Feb. 1989
Mitsubishi	Princes/Trex	Princes canned foods, Trex	£55m (estimate)	Feb. 1989
Allied Lyons	Chateau Latour (53.5%)	Chateau Latour	£56m	April 1989
Hillsdown	Premier Brands	Typhoo tea, Marvel, Chivers	£195m	May 1989
BSN	Nabicrisps	Jacobs, Smiths, Walkers	$2.5bn	June 1989
Pepsico	Smitpotate	Smiths, Walkers	$1.35bn	July 1989
Polly Peck	Del Monte (fresh fruit)	Del Monte	$875m	Aug. 1989
Cadbury Schweppes	Trebor	Trebor mints, Refreshers, Extra Strong mints	£110m	Sept. 1989
Cadbury Schweppes	Crush International	Crush, Gini, Hires	$220m	Oct. 1989

Source: Hill Samuel.

critical mass to compete effectively in an increasingly international marketplace.

2. A significant element influencing the bid premium which a predator might be prepared to pay was the perception of the value of the brand portfolio.

Furthermore, investors might reasonably have been expected to be alert to the potential for bid activity in the consumer goods sectors and for this to be reflected in the market capitalisations of those branded goods companies which, for one reason or another, were likely to be vulnerable.

There are, however, several reasons why stock markets have to date generally failed to reassess significantly the value of companies with brand portfolios. Firstly, an act of faith would be required to build into a share price a premium to reflect the possibility of a bid without having any indication of when or from whom the bid might come. Second, and probably more important, is the absence until recently of any objective yardstick to measure the value of brands in the same way that a company's other assets are valued.

Even with the emergence of a yardstick in the form of an independent valuation undertaken by specialists, the fairly small number of companies to have disclosed details of brand valuations in their published accounts has generally done little more than put a corporate toe in the water as they have valued (with the main exception of RHM) only recently acquired brands. On the basis of the small number of companies disclosing any details of brand values it is probably premature to draw any firm conclusions about whether or not brand valuations have influenced market capitalisations. What can be said, however, is that the increased prominence given to the role of brands in mergers and acquisitions means that the concept of a brand's value is now firmly embedded in the consciousness of investment bankers, investors and analysts.

Why RHM valued its brands

In 1988 RHM had sales of almost £1,700 million, profits of almost £160 million, fifty or so of the leading food brands in the British, Australian, New Zealand and 'Pacific rim' markets, almost 40,000 employees (90 per cent in Britain), a stock market capitalisation of £1,400 million but net assets of only £265 million. The reason for the low net asset figure was principally that the company had recently acquired another major foods group and had taken a substantial goodwill write-off.

In late 1988, even though the hostile Goodman Fielder Wattie bid had lapsed, RHM decided to include a formal valuation of its brands on its balance sheet. Its arguments were as follows:

1. It provided a more realistic picture of shareholders' funds.
2. It helped solve the goodwill write-off problem. Recognising the value of brands separately at the time of acquisition reduced the amount of goodwill that had to be written-off either directly to reserves or by amortisation over a number of years. Immediate write-off had a detrimental effect on consolidated reserves and confused the real value of the acquisition to the business whereas amortisation had a continuing adverse and unrealistic effect on future profits.
3. It allowed better comparisons between companies operating in similar markets or between companies with varying mixes of acquired and own-developed brands. (RHM saw no reason why acquired brands should be treated differently from 'home grown' ones since both can be equally valuable as assets to the company.)
4. It could assist capital-raising by reducing gearing ratios.
5. It could provide the basis for brands to be included as assets for Stock Exchange class-test purposes.

The valuation attached to RHM's brands was £678 million and the effect was to transform RHM's balance sheet with net assets rising from £265 million (in 1987) to £979 million (in 1988). Within a matter of days RHM announced that it had purchased Nabisco's British breakfast cereals interests (a move which would have been difficult without the brand valuation) and RHM's City image changed in a few months from that of a conservative, possibly even timid, miller and baker to that of a bold, pragmatic and successful foods group.

Possible ways to value brands

During their initial investigations RHM and Interbrand looked at various methods of valuation including the following:

Valuing brands

1. Valuation based on the aggregate cost of all marketing, advertising and research and development expenditure devoted to the brand over a stipulated period.
2. Valuation based on the premium pricing of a branded product over a non-branded product.
3. Valuation at market value.
4. Valuation based on various consumer-related factors such as esteem, recognition or awareness.
5. Valuation based on future earnings potential discounted to present day values.

Each of the above methods was rejected due to serious inherent drawbacks:

1. If the value of a brand is a function of the cost of its development failed brands may well be attributed high values. This method also ignores the current financial position of the brand and the legal aspects of protectability and registration.
2. The major benefits of branded products to manufacturers often relate to security and stability of future demand and effective utilisation of assets rather than to premium pricing. A strong brand which the retailer must stock due to customer demand provides a platform for the sale of additional products. It should also be remembered that many branded products (for example, a Mars Bar) have no generic equivalents. The value of a brand clearly cannot be determined by higher prices or margins alone.
3. Brands are not developed with the intention of trading in them, nor is there a ready market to determine such values. The market value of any asset will be the amount that a third party might reasonably pay for it. In the case of a brand, the market value may fluctuate widely depending on the identity and intended purpose of the interested party. Furthermore, the use of market value for balance sheet purposes is prohibited in Britain by the Companies Act.
4. A brand valuation based solely on consumer esteem or awareness factors would bear no relationship to commercial reality.
5. The determination of reliable forecast cash flows, future growth patterns and an appropriate discount rate is fraught with difficulty. Furthermore, for an asset to be capitalised on the balance sheet, the fundamental accounting concepts of prudence and consistency must

be applied. Any method relying on predicting future cash flow patterns cannot meet the requirements.

The methodology used by RHM and Interbrand (see Figure 16.1) computes the value of a brand by the application of an earning multiple to brand profitability, an overwhelmingly important factor in determining valuation. However, to arrive at a balance sheet value it is not enough merely to apply a simple multiplier to post tax profits. Firstly, not all of the profitability of a brand can necessarily be applied to a valuation of that brand. A brand may be essentially a commodity product, or may derive much of its profitability from its distribution system. The elements of profitability which do not result from the brand's identity must be excluded. Secondly, the value may be materially affected by using a single, possibly unrepresentative year's profit. RHM used a three year weighted average post tax profit figure to achieve this.

Brand strength

The determination of the multiple to be applied to brand profit is derived from an in-depth assessment of brand strength. This requires a detailed review of each brand, its positioning, the market in which it operates, competition, past performance, future plans, risks to the brand, etc. The brand strength is a composite of seven weighted factors, each of which is scored according to clearly established and consistent guidelines. These key factors are:

1. *Leadership*. A brand which leads its market sector is a more stable and valuable property than a brand lower down the order.
2. *Stability*. Long-established brands which command consumer loyalty and have become an integral part of the fabric of their markets are particularly valuable.
3. *Market*. Brands in markets such as food and drinks are intrinsically more valuable than brands in, for example, high-tech or clothing areas as these latter markets are more vulnerable to technological or fashion changes.
4. *Internationality*. Brands which are international are inherently more valuable than national or regional brands.
5. *Trend*. The overall long-term trend of the brand is an important

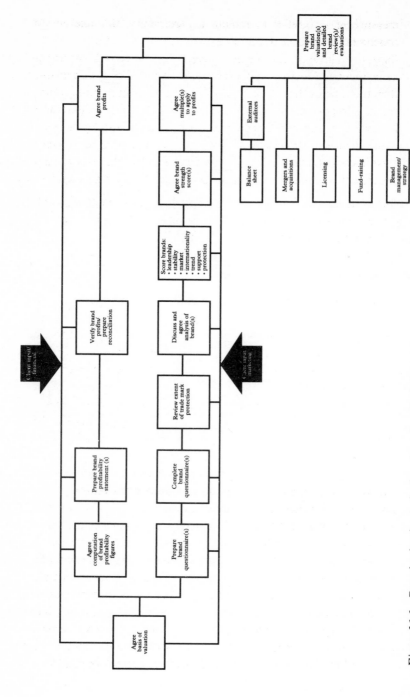

Figure 16.1 Brand valuation – the Interbrand methodology

measure of its ability to remain contemporary and relevant to consumers and hence of its value.

6. *Support.* Those brand names which have received consistent investment and focused support must be regarded as more valuable than those which have not. While the amount spent in supporting a brand is important the quality of this support is equally significant.

7. *Protection.* A registered trade mark is a statutory monopoloy in a name, device or in a combination of these two. Other protection may exist in common law, at least in certain countries. The strength and breadth of the brand's protection is critical in assessing its worth.

The brand is scored for each of these factors according to different weightings and the resultant total, the 'brand strength score', is expressed as a percentage.

The determination of the multiple

The relationship between brand strength as shown by the brand strength score and the multiple of earnings to be applied may be expressed graphically as an S curve. In fixing the multiples to be applied to the brand strength score the closest available analogy to the return from a notional perfect brand is the return from a risk-free investment. However, the perfect brand does not operate in a risk-free environment and the return from a risk-free investment is capital-free while part of a brand's earnings result from the capital employed in producing the product. Allowances for these factors must be taken into account in determining the multiple to be applied for a brand operating in a real business environment. Thus the highest multiple that can be applied will be somewhat lower than that for a risk-free investment and may vary from business to business and industry to industry.

The price/earnings (P/E) ratios of industries serving consumer goods sectors also provide an indicator of multiples that can reasonably be considered to apply to brands for balance sheet purposes. Thus the multiples at the high end of the scale should be greater than the average P/E ratio of the sector in which the company operates. Those at the low end of the scale will be below this average. In practice, the multiple which the Interbrand methodology attributes to a notional 'perfect' brand is twenty times average annual brand related earnings although the multiple attributed to an 'average' brand is substantially lower than this.

Amortisation

Generally brands have no fixed life and therefore RHM's capitalisation of brands has been made without any provision for amortisation. However, should a brand suffer a diminution in value, a provision for this reduction would be required. It may, however, be possible for any diminution to be offset by revaluation surpluses on other brands. Where it is clear that a brand has a finite life (e.g. a licensed brand) amortisation would of course be necessary.

Applications for brand valuation

The initial impetus for brand valuation has clearly been a desire by companies with weakened balance sheets as a result of post-acquisition goodwill write-offs to restore these balance sheets to a state which more sensibly and accurately reflects the underlying financial strength of the company. In doing so, however, they have stimulated a controversy which the chairman of the Accounting Standards Committee has described as 'the major accounting controversy of the last twenty years'. Many accountants, both in industry and private practice, have welcomed the inclusion of brands on the balance sheet and the stimulus which the brands debate has given to the profession to find a solution to the intangibles (or goodwill) problem. Others, however, especially those in the technical departments of the major accounting firms, have viewed the brands debate with something close to horror. In the summer of 1989 the London Business School entered the fray when it was retained by the Institute of Chartered Accountants in England and Wales to investigate the issue of brands on the balance sheet. While the LBS report encourages brand accounting for managment purposes it concludes that including brands on the balance sheet 'is potentially corrosive to the whole basis of financial reporting'. There is no doubt that the LBS report has lent strong support to the 'anti brands on the balance sheet' faction but those who support brands on the balance sheet show no signs whatsoever of conceding defeat, in fact the reverse. Coopers and Lybrand, for example, has attacked the conclusions of the London Business School in a most outspoken report.

While the accountancy debate continues, though, a host of applications have been developed for brand valuation which have nothing whatsoever to do with balance sheets. After all, once brands are specifically identified as valuable assets the management of those assets becomes much more critical. As brands are, for many companies, the engines of profitability, it is clear that companies will wish to understand brands and their performance better, will wish to establish brand values for licensing purposes (both internal and external), and will wish too when buying or selling brands or brand-rich companies to understand in detail the strengths and profitability of those brands.

Hitherto, companies have not understood their brands well and in only a minority of cases have companies employed any form of brand accounting. It seems likely that brand valuation, initially undertaken for reasons of balance sheet repair, will result in a major reappraisal of these assets and how they are accounted for and managed.

The future

The inclusion of brands on the balance sheet will undoubtedly continue to be a subject of major debate over the next two to three years. It is quite possible that the Accounting Standards Committee will seek to restrict the practice to acquired brands, it may even seek to outlaw it altogether. Users of accounts, however, are unlikely to stand by and allow a return to nineteenth century accounting when only things you can see, count and kick are allowed on the balance sheet. Whatever, therefore, is the short-term outcome of the current brands debate, in the medium to longer term it will surely result in a fundamental reappraisal of current accounting practices, probably on an international basis.

Perhaps most importantly, the brands debate is also leading to a fundamental reappraisal of brand management techniques and of the brand management system. It is clear that the principles of brand husbandry need to be much better understood, that information systems relating to brands need to be fundamentally overhauled in most cases and that the role of the brand manager needs to be redefined and integrated into the organisation at a much more senior level than is normally the case at present.

17

The future of branding

Modern branding has its roots in the nineteenth century but the major developments in branding over the last one hundred years are the increased emphasis upon the intangible components of a brand's personality, the extension of the branding concept to services as well as products, and the increased protection at law afforded to brand owners. In addition, it has been increasingly recognised that a corporation can be every bit as much a 'brand' as a product or service.

Future trends

All the above-mentioned trends are likely to continue for the foreseeable future and, in certain instances, will strengthen. The increased interest over the last thirty years in service brands, for example, will certainly become stronger as whole areas of service products which are not branded at present and which are provided by myriads of local suppliers with widely varying standards of quality and service (e.g. window cleaning) receive the 'branding treatment', possibly through franchise arrangements.

It also seems clear that the intangible components of brands will continue to be of critical importance. With increased wealth, the blurring of vocational roles between males and females, less compartmentalisation of life into activities and locations such as home, work and shopping, the increased dominance of wants over needs, and increased divergence in beliefs, values and attitudes, it seems certain that brands will increasingly be required with greater emotional appeal and greater variety.

In the area of law, it is also certain that legal systems will afford increasingly strong protection to owners of intellectual property. Countries such as Japan, the United States and those of Western Europe fully recognise that their prosperity depends not upon any unique access to manufacturing technology or sources of raw material but rather upon the skills, training, application and creativity of their inhabitants and business enterprises. Intellectual property legislation in these countries has been considerably strengthened in recent years and is viewed by legislators as an area of prime importance to international success. The United States has used the GATT (General Agreement on Tariffs and Trade) round of negotiations to link trading agreements with the extent to which countries control counterfeiting and enforce intellectual property rights. The World Intellectual Property Organisation (WIPO), part of the United Nations, is also active in strengthening intellectual property laws around the world and ensuring that they are enforced; and the European Economic Community is currently working as part of the 1992 initiative on a new trade mark system to embrace the whole of the EEC.

There are, however, in addition to these powerful trends, other new developments which are likely to have a significant impact upon branding in the foreseeable future.

Brand evaluation

Once the brand is recognised as a separable asset capable of producing cash flows in its own right, it becomes possible to treat the brand in many of the same ways as one treats any other form of valuable asset. The recent interest in brand valuation has already led to companies considering their brands in a totally new light. Several companies, for example, have instructed corporate finance advisers to dispose of unwanted brands for the best possible price in much the same way as they would previously have instructed them to dispose of an operating division, a subsidiary or a freehold property. Other companies, recognising a deficiency in their brand portfolios, are considering the acquisition of brands or branded goods companies.

Corporate raiders, too, now recognise the value of brands and the facts that they are transferable and command high prices in the marketplace. KKR's acquisition of RJR Nabisco and the Hoylake bid for BAT were both based, in substantial measure, on a fundamental reappraisal of underlying brand values.

The recognition of specific value in brands can also lead to other forms of corporate activity. Once brand value is recognised, and once it is recognised too that owners have specific title in their brands in the form of trade mark registrations, it becomes possible to mortgage or lease these brands and thus to use them as a form of security. In the United States, brand-based leases can be arranged at favourable rates and this facility will soon be available in the United Kingdom. It seems most likely, too, that major fund-raising in future by brand owners will be secured specifically on brands.

The licensing and franchising of brands will also become more common as brand owners seek to exploit more widely the equity in these valuable assets. It also seems inevitable that these two activities will become more expensive as their greater popularity with potential licensees and franchisees will enable brand owners to increase royalty rates.

Brand management

The brand management function in companies has traditionally been a training ground for high flyers whose main task has been that of maintaining a link between the company and its advertising and sales promotion agencies. The increased focus on, and interest in, brands seems certain to lead to a fundamental reappraisal of the role and status of brand management. Brand managers will be required to take a much more entrepreneurial view of their brands and will be held accountable for their profitability and for a proper return on brand assets, tangible and intangible. Several major companies are already redefining the marketing function and overhauling the brand management system. One major brand owner recently, when appointing a new director to the board, specifically recognised this by changing the title from Director of Marketing to Director of Brands.

The redefinition of the role of brand management and the elevation of brand management's status result in a need for new disciplines and new tools to allow better brand management to take place. Foremost among these is brand accounting, a practice which is currently followed by only

166

a handful of companies. As well as brand accounting, much better and more systematic brand planning will be required together with the formal tracking of all aspects of brand performance and not just market share.

The chairman of Verkade, one of Holland's major manufacturers of chocolate and biscuit products, recently remarked that only two years ago he saw himself as being primarily concerned with the financial strategy of the business. He has since totally redefined his role and now sees his primary responsibility as being the management and husbandry of the Verkade brand. The reappraisal of brand values and the specific attention which is being given to brands will inevitably mean that this process will be matched in other companies which will adopt an increasingly brand-centric approach to their activities.

Brand extension versus new brand development

It has recently been suggested by several commentators, particularly in the United States, that the days of new brand development are over and that no company would ever again be so foolhardy as to attempt it. While it seems clear that, given the choice between new brand development and brand extension, brand owners must give serious consideration to the extension route, nonetheless in very many instances the option of extending will not exist. Although a company may prefer to extend its brands or to acquire existing ones, if these routes are not available to it then it may have no choice but to develop a new brand. A specific recognition of the reasons for new brand development and of the risks involved is important to success as many brand failures have occurred simply because the company had no notion that it was engaging in a risky activity. There are, in addition, a number of strategies which can be used to reduce the risk of new brand development such as the exploration of other markets for new brand ideas and more meaningful market research.

Internationalisation

Major international brand owners have, during the 1980s, substantially increased their hold on world markets both through the winning of larger market shares and through the acquisition of other branded goods businesses. In the EC, for example, in the run up to 1992 and the completion of the internal market, major brand owners have looked anxiously at establishing a powerful brand position across Europe because they have recognised that one of the implications of a larger trading group and of better communications will be the increased dominance of the more powerful international brands. This process is likely to continue for the foreseeable future though new niche brands, often those which were originally based on local tastes and habits, will constantly be introduced and will provide consumers with continuing variety and interest.

Own label brands

In Britain at least, own label is becoming a strategy for retailers to create loyalties to the retailer's brand rather than to manufacturers' brands; thus in many instances own label brands are not so much inexpensive versions of manufacturers' brands as superior alternatives. Although in the past manufacturers became concerned about the growth of own label, more recently they have come to regard own label brands as being merely a feature of a more varied brand landscape and not as posing any fundamental threat. Manufacturers have taken particular heart from the fact that own label brands appear in recent years to have settled down at a market share of around 30–35 per cent, at least in such sectors as food and drink.

While it seems clear that there is no prospect of own label brands destroying manufacturers' brands, if only because many smaller retailers are unable to follow the own label route, nonetheless there seems no reason why manufacturers' brands should have a divine right to the majority of any market. Own label brands have gained share because they are innovative, attractive, well packaged, well priced and offer the consumer satisfactions which manufacturers' brands do not. Manufacturers need to respond to this phenomenon in a much more constructive way than they have done to date. They need to be more innovative, they need to reduce the costs of new product development and launch, and they also need considerably to reduce the timescale required to bring new products to market.

Furthermore, the phenomenon of own label, which is particularly well established in Britain, seems likely to become more powerfully established in markets such as the United States as integrated national retail chains develop at the expense of local or regional operators.

Appendix: Trade marks advertised prior to registration in the official *UK Trade Marks Journal*

1,284,831. 14 October 1986. (Class 3)

XI'A XI'ANG

Registration of this mark shall give no right to the exclusive use of the letters 'XI'A'.

Soaps, perfumes, essential oils, cosmetics, non-medicated toilet preparations, non-medicated preparations for the care of the skin and body; all included in Class 3.

Charles of The Ritz Group Limited, 40 West 57th Street, New York, New York 10019, United States of America.

Agent: Graham Watt & Co., Riverhead, Sevenoaks, Kent TN13 2BN.

1,311,520. 29 May 1987. (Class 3)

Miami Dolphins

Registration of this mark shall give no right to the exclusive use of the letter 'M' and the word 'Miami'.

Non-medicated toilet preparations; perfumes; eau de cologne; toilet waters; pre-shave and aftershave preparations and substances; soaps; shampoos; foamable preparations for the bath; preparations for the hair; dentifrices; deodorants for personal use; antiperspirants; preparations for the use in suntanning; cleaning and non-medicated preparations; all impregnated into tissues and into pads and for personal use; all included in Class 3.

N.F.L. Properties (UK) Limited, 18 Bedford Row, London WC1R 4EJ.

Agent: Urquhart-Dykes & Lord, 91 Wimpole Street, London W1M 8AH.

1,348,742. 5 July 1988. (Class 3)

Soil removing preparations and cleaning preparations, all for use on fabrics or the like materials, all included in Class 3.

Frank Lucenta, 9504 East 55th Street, Tulsa, State of Oklahoma 74145, United States of America.

Agent: D. Young & Co., 10 Staple Inn, London WC1V 7PD.

1,351,423. 18 July 1988. (Class 6)

TALOS

Tubes included in Class 6 made wholly or principally of metal.

Halcor Metal Processing Company S.A., 115 Kifissias Avenue, Athens 11524, Greece.

Agent: Carpmaels & Ransford, 43 Bloomsbury Square, London WC1A 2RA.

1,308,119. 24 April 1987. (Class 7)

MARS

Modular Automation Robot Systems

Registration of this mark shall give no right to the exclusive use of the words 'Modular Automation Robot Systems'.

Robotic arms and end effectors, all for use in flexible manufacture and included in Class 7.

Research Development Associates Ltd., Business & Technology Centre, Bessemer Drive, Stevenage, Herts SG1 2DX.

1,335,750. 17 February 1988. (Class 7)

TARDIS

To be associated with No. 1,335,749 (5784, 4085).

Casings, parts and fittings, all included in Class 7 for machines.

Klockner-Moeller Limited, P.O. Box 35, Gatehouse Close, Aylesbury, Bucks HP19 3DH.

Agent: Marks & Clerk, 57–60 Lincoln's Inn Fields, London WC2A 3LS.

1,343,662. 6 May 1988. (Class 7)

To be associated with No. 1,324,790 (5782, 3764).

Airbrushes and parts and fittings therefor, all included in Class 7.

Appendix

Eastman Technology Incorporated, 343 State Street, Rochester, New York 14650, United States of America.
Agent: J. B. Draper, Kodak Ltd., P.O. Box 66, Station Road, Hemel Hempstead, Hertfordshire HP1 1JU.

B1,296,340.   23 December 1986.   (Class 9)

The transliteration of the Chinese characters appearing in the mark is 'Kamg Jia', meaning 'Healthy and Beautiful'.
Registration of this mark shall give no right to the exclusive use of the letters 'KK'.
Sound or video recording and reproducing apparatus and installations; television apparatus; radios incorporating clocks; electronic apparatus and instruments; parts and fittings for all the aforesaid goods; all included in Class 9.
Kwong Ming Overseas Chinese Electronics Industrial Ltd., Shaho Ind Area, Shenzhen City, Guangdong Province, China.
Agent: Withers & Rogers, 4 Dyer's Buildings, Holborn, London EC1N 2JT.

B1,324,103.   14 October 1987.   (Class 9)

HOTBOT

Electrical hot water bottles included in Class 9.
Reginald Charles David Vint, The Heritage, Old Mill Lane, Bray, Maidenhead, Berkshire SL6 2QL.
Agent: Potts, Kerr & Co., P.O. Box 688, Ascot, Berkshire SL5 8YT.

B1,339,284.   18 March 1988.   (Class 9)

To be associated with No. B1,339,282 (5783, 3945).

Apparatus and instruments, all for the processing, storage, retrieval, communication, display, input, output and print-out of data; computers, computer terminals and printers therefor; video display units; floppy disc driving apparatus; modems; apparatus and instruments, all for detecting, monitoring, testing and measuring; electronic security apparatus; telecommunications apparatus and instruments; surveillance apparatus; electronic apparatus and instruments, all for recognising digital and analogue codes; control apparatus for all the aforesaid goods; cards, discs, tapes, wires, microchips and electronic circuits, all for the recordal of data; parts and fittings included in Class 9 for all the aforesaid goods; computer programmes and computer software; all included in Class 9.

Octocom Systems Inc., 255 Ballardvale Street, Wilmington, Massachusetts 01887, United States of America.

Agent: R. G. C. Jenkins & Co., 26 Caxton Street, London SW1H 0RJ.

1,349,830. 30 June 1988. (Class 9)

BLUE MOVES

Phonograph records, cassettes, cartridges, magnetic tapes, optical discs; apparatus and materials, all for the storage of data for the reproduction of sound or images; all included in Class 9.

Blue Moves Limited, 46 Willow Street, London EC2A 4BH.

Agent: Reginald W. Barker & Co., 13 Charterhouse Square, London EC1M 6BA.

1,309,917. 14 May 1987. (Class 10)

AEROLIN 400

To be associated with No. 1,309,915 (5757, 426) and another.

Inhalation devices included in Class 10 for the administration of medicines.

Riker Laboratories Inc., 19901 Nordhoff Street, Northridge, California 91324, United States of America.

Agent: Stevens, Hewlett & Perkins, 5–9 Quality Court, Chancery Lane, London WC2A 1HZ.

Appendix

B1,274,348. 13 August 1986. (Class 11)

 THE NATIONAL TRUST COUNTRY HOUSE COLLECTION

THE NATIONAL TRUST
COUNTRY HOUSE COLLECTION

Application under Section 21(2) for a series of three marks.

Advertised before acceptance by reason of special circumstances. Section 18(1) (proviso).

Registration of this mark shall give no right to the exclusive use of the words 'Country House Collection'.

Table lamps and lampshades, all included in Class 11 and for sale in England, Wales and Northern Ireland.

The National Trust (Enterprises) Limited, 42 Queen Anne's Gate, London SW1H 9AS.

Agent: F. J. Cleveland & Company, 40–43 Chancery Lane, London WC2A 1JQ.

1,343,205. 30 April 1988. (Class 12)

VOGUE

Advertised before acceptance. Section 18(1) (proviso).

Motor land vehicles and parts and fittings therefor, all included in Class 12.

Land Rover UK Limited, 11 Strand, London WC2N 5JT.

Agent: The Rover Group, Patent, Trade Mark and Licensing Department, Cowley Body Plant, Oxford OX4 5NL.

B1,220,161. 5 June 1984. (Class 15)

Registration of this mark shall give no right to the exclusive use of the words 'My Melody'.

To be associated with No. 1,220,159 (5702, 2823) and others.

Castanets, harmonicas, music boxes, cases for musical instruments.

Kabushiki Kaishi Sanrio (Sanrio Company Limited), 6th Floor TOC Building, 7-22-17 Nishigotanda, Shinagawa-ku, Tokyo, Japan.

Agent: D. Young & Co., 10 Staple Inn, London WC1V 7RD.

B1,290,306. 7 November 1986. (Class 16)

MASTERMIND

Advertised before acceptance. Section 18(1) (proviso).

Printed publications included in Class 16, all relating to general knowledge.

The British Broadcasting Corporation, Broadcasting House, Portland Place, London W1A 1AA.

Agent: Frank B. Dehn & Co., Imperial House, 15–19 Kingsway, London WC2B 6UZ.

1,314,473. 1 July 1987. (Class 16)

UNCLE

Printed matter, instructional and teaching materials, all relating to computer programs; paper tapes and cards, all for the recordal and storage of computer programs; all included in Class 16.

United Kingdom Atomic Energy Authority, 11 Charles II Street, London SW1Y 4QP.

Agent: J. E. Alderman, Patents Branch, United Kingdom Atomic Energy Authority, 11 Charles II Street, London SW1Y 4QP.

B1,274,514. 15 August 1986. (Class 18)

Handbags, purses and pocket wallets; bags adapted for campers and for climbers; beach bags, game bags, shopping bags, travelling bags, valises and sling bags for carrying infants; school bags and satchels; haversacks, rucksacks, brief cases, card cases, music cases and cases of leather or leatherboard; boxes; umbrellas and umbrella covers; all included in Class 18; but not including travelling bags, school bags and satchels, haversacks or rucksacks, all in the form of bears.

Unilever PLC., Port Sunlight, Wirral, Merseyside.

Agent: Blackfriars Trade Mark Services, P.O. Box 68, Blackfriars, London EC4P 4BQ.

B1,294,908. 4 December 1986. (Class 21)

Registration of this mark shall give no right to the exclusive use of the letter 'W' and the word 'Wimbledon'.

To be associated with No. B1,294,906 (5757, 457).

Small domestic utensils and containers, combs and sponges; glassware, porcelain and earthenware; sculptures; figurines; all included in Class 21.

The All England Lawn Tennis Club (Wimbledon) Limited, Church Road, Wimbledon, London SW19.

Agent: Boult, Wade & Tennant, 27 Furnival Street, London EC4A 1PQ.

1,307,456. 15 April 1987. (Class 25)

The mark, here depicted in heraldic shading, is limited to the colours red and blue as shown in the representation on the form of application.
To be associated with No. 1,307,454 (5774, 2621) and others.
Articles of outerclothing; footwear; pants; leotards; tights; all included in Class 25.
Pepsico, Inc., Purchase, New York 10577, United States of America.
Agent: D. Young & Co., 10 Staple Inn, London WC1V 7RD.

B1,349,550.   29 June 1988.   (Class 28)

THE ART OF LOVE

Registration of this mark shall give no right to the exclusive use of the word 'Love'.
Toys, novelties and games; all included in Class 28.
Humatt Limited, 41 Shirley Street, London E16 1HU.
Agent: Graham Jones & Company, 77 Beaconsfield Road, Blackheath, London SE3 7LG.

1,228,517.   18 October 1984.   (Class 31)

Use claimed from the year 1978. Section 12(2).
Agricultural, horticultural and forestry products; grains; all included in Class 31; fresh fruits and fresh vegetables; live plants and natural flowers.
Fargro Limited, Canterbury Road, Worthing, Sussex BN13 1AP.
Agent: Marks & Clerk, 57–60 Lincoln's Inn Fields, London WC2A 3LS.

1,350,430.   1 July 1988.   (Class 31)

BALLERINA

It is a condition of registration that the mark shall not be used as a varietal name.

Apple trees and parts thereof, propagation materials derived from all the aforesaid goods; apples; all included in Class 31.

Columnar Trees Limited, Newton Hall, Newton, Cambridge, CB2 5PS.

Agent: Blackfriars Trade Mark Services, P.O. Box 68, Blackfriars, London EC4P 4BQ.

1,315,325. 8 July 1987. (Class 32)

OLD THUMPER

Strong ale included in Class 32.

Ringwood Brewery Ltd, 138 Christchurch Road, Ringwood, Hants BH24 3AP.

1,298,398. 21 January 1987. (Class 35)

Export and import agency services and advertising services relating thereto; all included in Class 35.

V/O 'Exportkhleb', Smolenskaja-Sennaja, 32/34 Moscow, 121200, United Soviet Socialist Republic.

Agent: Marks & Clerk, 57–60 Lincoln's Inn Fields, London WC2A 3LS.

B1,317,107. 28 July 1987. (Class 35)

TURQUANDS BARTON MAYHEW

Registration of this mark shall give no right to the exclusive use of the words 'Barton' and 'Mayhew'.

Accountancy services; business planning and business research services; management consultations; all included in Class 35.

Ernst & Whinney International, 18th Floor, 1285 Avenue of the Americas, New York, NY 10019, United States of America.
Agent: Markforce Associates, 40 Long Acre, London WC2E 9JT.

B1,299,495. 31 January 1987. (Class 42)

Nurse-Call

Registration of this mark shall give no right to the exclusive use of the word 'Nurse-Call'.
Nursing services included in Class 42.
Nurse-Call Limited, 16 Forest Lane, Martlesham Heath, Ipswich, Suffolk IP5 7ST.
Agent: William Jones, CPA, Willow Lane House, Willow Lane, Norwich NR2 1EU.

1,344,482. 14 May 1988. (Class 42)

OINK

Catering services included in Class 42.
High Birch Poultry Farm Limited, High Birch Road, Weeley Heath, Nr. Clacton-on-Sea, Essex CO16 9BU.
Agent: Sanderson & Co., 34 East Stockwell Street, Colchester, Essex CO1 1ST.

Bibliography

Bureau, J. R. 1981. *Branding Management: Planning and Control*. London: Macmillan.

Burgelman, R. A. and L. R. Sayles. 1986. *Inside Corporate Innovation: Strategy, Structure and Managerial Skills*. New York: Free Press.

Buzzell, R. D. and B. T. Gale. 1987. *The PIMS Principles: Linking Strategy to Performance*. New York: Free Press.

Campbell, A. 1983. *The Designer's Handbook*. London: Macdonald.

Davidson, J. H. 1987. *Offensive Marketing: Or How to Make Your Competitors Follow* (2nd edn). Harmondsworth: Penguin.

Hurlburt, A. 1982. *The Design Concept*. New York: Watson-Guptill.

Lorenz, C. 1986. *The Design Dimension: Product Strategy and the Challenge of Global Marketing*. Oxford: Basil Blackwell.

Murphy, J. (ed.) 1987. *Branding: A Key Marketing Tool*. London: Macmillan; New York: McGraw-Hill.

Murphy, J. and M. Rowe. 1988. *How to Design Trademarks and Logos*. Oxford: Phaidon Press; Cincinnati, Ohio: Northlight Books.

Murphy, J. (ed.) 1989. *Brand Valuation: A True and Fair View*. London: Hutchinson.

Index

accounting in brand management, 104, 108, 149–57, 162, 163
Accounting Standards Committee, 154, 162, 163
acquisitions and mergers, 23–4, 151, 152–7
advertising, need for, 21, 110
Airwick Industries, 149
amortisation, 157, 162
Anheuser-Busch (company), 147
Anti-counterfeiting Group, 135
appeal
  consumer, 2, 4, 6, 23
  international, 74, 76
Apple computers, 56
assets, brands as, 23–4, 152–3, 156, 157, 163, 165–6
Australia
  brand valuation, 149, 150–1
  franchising in, 144

'balance sheet/brand valuation' debate, 150–2, 162, 163
Bass Red Triangle, 18
BAT (British American Tobacco), 166
Beecham Group, 111–12
Booz Allen & Hamilton, 28–9
BP Chemicals, 59
brand
  'blueprint', 106–7
  equity *see* equity
  extension, 13–14, 73–4, 111–14, 167
  failure, 20–1, 29
  image, 10–13
  personality, 65, 70, 74, 76–7, 112–13
  search, 33–5

strength, 159, 161
brand-centricity, 104–5
Bristol Myers Co., 9
British Airways, 93
British Telecom, 53, 85
Brylcreem, 13, 111, 112
buying consortia, 66

catering chains, 42, 144
character merchandising, 142–3
Ciba-Geigy, 149
Coca-Cola, 9, 19, 90, 107
  and brand personality, 1–2, 3
  and international branding, 23, 117, 120
  licensing, 141
  logo design, 84, 96
coined names, 80–2
collateral, use of brands as, 151, 152
collateral exploitation or licensing, 141, 142
communication, corporate, need for, 51–2, 53, 93
communications and international branding, 23, 118
competition, 5–6
competitive depositioning, 6, 7
computerised name generation, 77, 78
confidence, consumer, 3, 8, 21–2, 40, 51
consortia formation, 66
consultants, use of, 26
consumer(s)
  appeal, 2, 4, 6, 23
  choice, 19–20, 21–2
  confidence, 3, 8, 21–2, 40, 51
  industrial, 58–9, 60
  loyalty, 7, 9, 14, 55, 101, 105

183

Index

Index

Index